insight text guide

Virginia Lee

The Dressmaker

Rosalie Ham

First published in 2021, reprinted in 2022.

Insight Publications Pty Ltd
3/350 Charman Road
Cheltenham VIC 3192
Australia
Tel: +61 3 8571 4950
Fax: +61 3 8571 0257
Email: books@insightpublications.com.au

www.insightpublications.com.au

A catalogue record for this book is available from the National Library of Australia

Rosalie Ham's The Dressmaker / Virginia Lee

Virginia Lee asserts the moral right to be identified as the author of this work.

ISBNs:
9781922525406 (print)
9781922525413 (digital)
9781922525420 (bundle: print + digital)

Cover design by Melisa Paredes

Printed by Markono Print Media Pte Ltd

contents

CHARACTER MAP

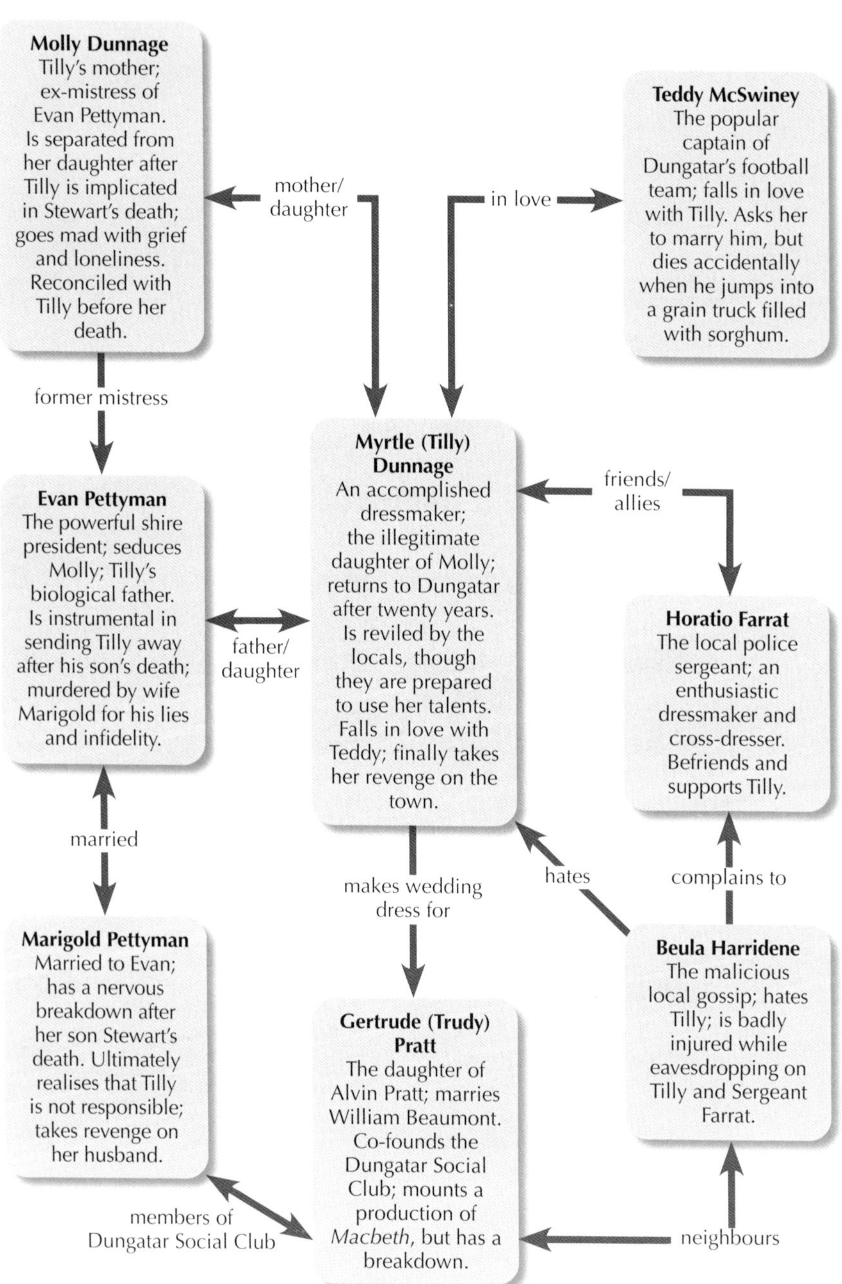

OVERVIEW

About the author

Rosalie Ham is a contemporary Australian writer of novels, plays and short stories. Born in 1955, she grew up on a farm in Jerilderie, New South Wales, and has drawn extensively on this farming background in her writing. Four of her novels are set in small rural communities and explore the social dynamics between people living in this – potentially claustrophobic – context.

Ham wrote *The Dressmaker*, her debut novel, as part of a writing course at RMIT University. It was first published in 2000 to commercial and critical acclaim; the novel was short-listed for the Christina Stead Prize for Fiction at the 2001 New South Wales Premier's Literary Awards and was a finalist for the State Library of Victoria's Most Popular Novel (2007). It has also been made into a successful film.

Ham has written four other novels: *Summer at Mount Hope* (2005), *There Should Be More Dancing* (2011) and *The Year of the Farmer* (2018). In 2020, *The Dressmaker's Secret* – a sequel to *The Dressmaker* – was published, which picks up Tilly Dunnage's story two years after she leaves Dungatar.

Synopsis

Thirty-year-old Myrtle (Tilly) Dunnage returns to her home town of Dungatar after an absence of twenty years. She has lived and worked in Europe as a successful dressmaker, training under some of Europe's finest couturiers. Tilly finds her mother, Molly, living in squalor and ostracised by the town.

Tilly's own memories of Dungatar are painful. As a ten-year-old, she was implicated in the death of a fellow pupil, Stewart Pettyman. Stewart, the son of the powerful shire president and Tilly's biological father, habitually bullied her about her illegitimacy. In the incident that resulted in his death, Stewart charged at her headfirst and, when Tilly stepped aside, he crashed into a brick wall and broke his neck. Blamed by Evan Pettyman for his son's death, Tilly was separated from her mother and sent away to school in Melbourne.

At first, Dungatar treats Tilly's homecoming with suspicion and hostility. Her only friends are Sergeant Farrat, the policeman, and Teddy McSwiney, the popular football hero. The latter falls in love with Tilly and, despite her caution, she starts to reciprocate his feelings. After making a wedding gown for Gertrude Pratt, a local girl, Tilly wins grudging acceptance in the town and builds up a thriving dressmaking business.

Gertrude – now Mrs William Beaumont and known as Trudy – establishes the Dungatar Social Club with her mother-in-law, Elsbeth. A number of events are planned, including a ball, for which Tilly makes the dresses. Tilly attends the ball with Teddy, but is shunned by the other guests. Afterwards, Tilly confides in Teddy about her past and the pair decide to marry. In a foolhardy gesture designed to reassure Tilly that they have nothing to fear, Teddy jumps into a grain truck that he mistakenly thinks is full of wheat, and suffocates. In spite of Sergeant Farrat's best efforts, Tilly is blamed by the townspeople, who again turn their backs on the Dunnages. A new dressmaker, Una Pleasance, is brought to town.

Approximately a year after Teddy's death, Molly has a strange dream about a baby. Tilly tells her mother that she had a son in Paris, Pablo, who died at seven months. Mother and daughter are reconciled. Shortly afterwards, Molly has a bad fall as the result of a stroke, and dies. Distraught, Tilly vows revenge against the townspeople for all the needless suffering they have caused the Dunnages.

As Una Pleasance's shortcomings as a dressmaker have become painfully clear, the Social Club asks Tilly to make the costumes for the forthcoming drama eisteddfod. Seeing an opportunity, Tilly encourages Trudy to choose ludicrous baroque costumes for Dungatar's production of *Macbeth*.

A series of bizarre – in some cases, fatal – accidents involving several of the town's prominent citizens, including Evan Pettyman, lead to the arrival of an investigating district inspector. In the meantime, rehearsals for the play go from bad to worse, with director Trudy becoming increasingly irrational. On the day of the eisteddfod, the cast travel to Winyerp without her; not surprisingly, their performance is a disaster. In their absence, Tilly deliberately sets fire to her own house, but makes sure that the blaze will spread. She then leaves for Melbourne. When the townspeople return, Dungatar has been burnt to the ground.

Character summaries

Myrtle (Tilly) Dunnage

The protagonist of the novel, Tilly is thirty years old and returns to her home town of Dungatar to assist her ailing mother, Molly. A trained dressmaker, she starts designing and making dresses for the local women and falls in love with Teddy McSwiney. However, her already fraught relationship with the town sours further after his accidental death. Ultimately, Tilly has her revenge.

Molly Dunnage

Molly is likely in her late fifties or early sixties. As a young woman she was seduced by Evan Pettyman and bore an illegitimate child, Myrtle (Tilly). She has been reviled and shunned by the town ever since her daughter was sent away. Initially, she does not respond well to Tilly's attempts to look after her.

Teddy McSwiney

The eldest child of the large McSwiney family, Teddy is the local football hero. He falls in love with Tilly and plans to marry her, but dies in a tragic accident.

Edward McSwiney

Teddy's father Edward is Dungatar's night cart man. He and his family live at the base of The Hill beside the tip.

Mae McSwiney

Mae is Teddy's mother and married to Edward. She gave Molly some support before Tilly's arrival.

Barney McSwiney

The second son of the McSwiney clan, Barney is slightly disabled with a withered leg and a club foot.

Horatio Farrat

The local police sergeant, originally from Melbourne, Farrat enjoys sewing and cross-dresses in private. He becomes Tilly's friend and ally.

Evan Pettyman

Pettyman is Dungatar's shire president and Tilly's biological father. A chronic womaniser who manipulates his wife, Marigold, he was also instrumental in separating Tilly from her mother. Justice, in the form of Tilly and Marigold, catches up with him.

Marigold Pettyman

Marigold is Evan Pettyman's long-suffering wife and the mother of their deceased son, Stewart.

Stewart Pettyman

The son of Evan and Marigold, and Tilly's half-brother, Stewart was killed as a child when he ran headlong into a brick wall while trying to assault Tilly.

Gertrude (Trudy) Pratt

Gertrude, daughter of Alvin and Muriel Pratt, marries William Beaumont, changes her name to Trudy and forms the Dungatar Social Club. She directs the Club's production of *Macbeth* for the drama eisteddfod.

Alvin Pratt

Alvin is the owner and proprietor of A and M Pratt, Merchant Supplies, the profitable general store that supplies all goods to the town – from food to hardware.

Muriel Pratt

Muriel is Alvin's wife and Trudy's mother.

Elsbeth Beaumont

Elsbeth is the owner of Windswept Crest estate and the leader of the Dungatar social set. She is the widow of Bill Beaumont, a grazier, and the mother of William and Mona. Elsbeth forms the Social Club with her daughter-in-law, Trudy.

William Beaumont

Elsbeth's son William is heir to Windswept Crest. He marries Gertrude Pratt.

Mona Beaumont

Mona, Elsbeth's daughter, marries Lesley Muncan.

Fred Bundle

The local publican, owner of the Station Hotel, Fred is married to Purl.

Purl Bundle

Purl runs the pub with her husband, Fred.

Reginald Blood

Reg is the butcher who works at Pratts Store. He plays in the local band and his affair with Faith O'Brien is common knowledge.

Mr Almanac

As Dungatar's chemist (pharmacist), in the absence of a town doctor Mr Almanac is the dispenser of all medical treatment. He is married to Irma and suffers from advanced Parkinson's disease.

Irma Almanac

Irma suffers from arthritic pain. During Tilly's absence, she discreetly sent food to Molly.

Faithful (Faith) O'Brien

Faith is the lead singer in the O'Brien Brothers Band. She is married to Hamish, but having an affair with Reg.

Hamish O'Brien

Hamish, the stationmaster, is married to Faith and also plays in the band.

Septimus Crescant

Hamish's drinking companion, Septimus is the founder of the Flat Earth Society.

Beula Harridene

Beula is the local gossip. She hates Tilly and tries to undermine her in every way, but her malicious snooping comes to an unexpected end.

Lois Pickett

Beula's friend Lois is the mother of Nancy and Bobby. She cleans house for Irma Almanac.

Nancy Pickett

Nancy works for Mr Almanac and is in a relationship with Ruth Dimm.

Bobby Pickett

Nancy's younger brother Bobby plays football for the Dungatar team.

Scotty Pullit

Scotty also plays football for Dungatar, as well as distilling the local firewater.

Ruth Dimm

Ruth, Dungatar's postmistress and part-time librarian, is in a relationship with Nancy.

Prudence Dimm

Ruth's sister Prudence is the teacher who runs the local school. She taught the young Tilly.

Lesley Muncan

The impecunious (poor) equestrian Lesley is offered a job at Windswept Crest then marries Mona Beaumont.

Una Pleasance

Elsbeth Beaumont's cousin Una is a dressmaker who is brought to Dungatar by the Social Club as a replacement for Tilly. She becomes Evan Pettyman's mistress.

BACKGROUND & CONTEXT

Australia in the 1950s

The Dressmaker is set in the early 1950s when Australia was still a very young nation, geographically remote and culturally unsophisticated. Commercial air travel was uncommon and sea voyages to Europe or America took weeks or even months, so travelling extensively overseas, as Tilly Dunnage has done, was rare.

Australia was entering into a period of prosperity and transition. The huge influx of postwar migrants brought economic growth and ethnic diversity, as well as fresh attitudes. America's emergence as the dominant postwar power meant that there was a cultural and political shift away from Great Britain, towards the United States. American popular culture was making its mark through cinema and music. In the text, Tilly listens to Billie Holiday; there is also reference to JD Salinger's novel *The Catcher in the Rye*, and the musical *South Pacific*. In an effort to impress Tilly, Teddy sports a look – Levi jeans, white T-shirt and leather jacket – made popular by American film stars such as Marlon Brando and James Dean: 'His hair shone with Brylcream [*sic*] and he had developed an insolent, upper body lean and matching pout' (p.156).

Although the text includes little mention of external affairs or the outside world, some details help to contextualise the story. For example, Teddy references the fact that the famous Irish playwright George Bernard Shaw has died – this was in November 1950. A few months later, Teddy takes Tilly and Molly to see the film *Sunset Boulevard*, which was released in August 1950, but would not have hit Australian cinemas – especially a cultural backwater like Dungatar – until 1951.

In the 1950s, gender roles were clearly delineated. Women of this generation were largely dependent on men, economically and socially; indeed, many married women were legally required to give up the jobs they had before marriage. Few women went on to further study after school or had ambitions beyond marriage – Gertrude Pratt is typical. While the novel does show women at work, this is either in a family-run business – such as Pratts – or a reflection of their spinster status.

Australia prided itself on its egalitarianism, but social divisions were prevalent. These are evident in *The Dressmaker*. As Dungatar's night cart man, Edward McSwiney is at the bottom of the social pecking order. Conversely, Elsbeth Beaumont is seen to be of superior social standing because she married a grazier's son and owns land. Even though Alvin Pratt is well-off, Elsbeth objects to William's marriage on the basis that Gertrude's father is a shop owner.

The novel also references aspects of Australian society peculiar to the times. For example, restrictive licensing laws meant that hotels were obliged to close at six o'clock. However, Sergeant Farrat turns a blind eye to the law and, after giving Fred Bundle a perfunctory hint to wind up, he leaves the Station Hotel knowing full well that the Saturday-night drinking will continue.

The wheatbelt

The fictitious town of Dungatar and its neighbours, Winyerp and Itheca, are located in the Victorian wheatbelt. This region, north-west of Melbourne, is named for the crop that, historically, has been one of Australia's main exports; it also produces coarse grains such as sorghum, oilseeds and legumes. In *The Dressmaker*, 'the farms around Dungatar are golden seas of wheat', whereas 'Winyerp sits ... in the middle of an undulating brown blanket' of sorghum (p.126). Ham describes the seasonal process whereby the trains pull into the towns and their empty trucks are filled with grain from the silos. The engines then tow the trucks away – sometimes up to fifty at a time – 'brimming with dusty gold and brown seed' (p.127). To Tilly, who has grown up in the area, the cycle is reassuringly familiar, 'a map' (p.127).

Fashion in the 1950s

'Haute couture' is a French term, literally meaning 'high fashion'. Exclusive, custom-made clothes are designed and created for individual clients, sometimes taking up to 700 hours to complete. They are generally sewn by hand, using expensive, often unusual fabrics. In the 1950s, considered a 'golden age' in fashion, approximately 15 000 women in the world wore couture; in the twenty-first century, it caters for an increasingly small clientele of about 2000.

Postwar Paris was the undisputed epicentre of fashion and the home of many celebrated couturiers. *The Dressmaker* refers to actual designers and fashion houses, and Tilly has learnt from some of the masters. In particular, she was recommended to the House of Balenciaga by designer Madeleine Vionnet, with whom she had a personal relationship. Cristóbal Balenciaga was a masterful tailor who created sculptural effects with fabric that altered the silhouette of a woman's body. His designs liberated women from corseted waists, allowing more freedom of movement.

Many of Tilly's designs show the influence of her mentor. The grey linen tunic she designs for Muriel Pratt – 'well tailored, chic and practical' (pp.135–6) – evokes Balenciaga, while Sergeant Farrat praises Tilly's designs as showing 'the structure of Balenciaga, the simplicity of Chanel, the drapery of Vionnet and the art of Delaunay' (p.167).

By contrast, Australian fashion was not only derivative but, in the pre-internet age, was also up to twelve months behind Europe. The only way Australian buyers could access European collections was to physically attend the shows. Designs and fabrics were then shipped back to Australia where they were copied by local fashion houses and dressmakers. In Melbourne, establishments at the 'Paris' end of Collins Street – such as the boutique Le Louvre and the exclusive department store Georges – promoted themselves as exponents of high fashion. However, by the time the product reached suburban stores that catered to the cheaper end of the market – such as Rockmans – they bore little resemblance to the original European designs in quality or cut.

GENRE, STRUCTURE & LANGUAGE

Genre

The Dressmaker is a modern Gothic novel, in that it incorporates some of the elements of classic Gothic fiction, albeit in a twentieth-century setting. There is a blend of horror and romance, a 'cursed' protagonist (in this case, a heroine), and a number of characters who evince a disturbed psyche. Ham builds an atmosphere of foreboding, and the text culminates in a series of violent, macabre 'accidents' that are predicated on karma.

In this sense, the novel is also an acerbic morality fable. The 'sour people of Dungatar' (p.236) are punished for their vindictiveness against the Dunnages. Tilly engineers a decisive revenge against the town, while those individuals who have behaved with particular cruelty – Evan Pettyman, Beula Harridene and Mr Almanac – are singled out for special punishment.

Further, *The Dressmaker* is an evocation of Australian country life in the 1950s. Many of the characters border on caricature – larger-than-life creations that often represent a 'type'. A number of these are recognisable, such as the jovial publican, his expansive wife, the town busybody and the paternal policeman. The Saturday-morning cake stall and the Saturday-afternoon football match are equally familiar. The pub is the social heart of the town, and football is the glue that binds the townspeople together.

Into this otherwise unremarkable context, Ham introduces an element of magic realism. The supernatural intrudes when Molly inexplicably dreams of her grandson, Pablo, on the same night that Tilly has her own dream. This mysterious coincidence becomes the narrative device through which the two women are genuinely reconciled.

Structure

The novel has a linear structure, within which Ham includes a number of flashbacks to Tilly's childhood that recall relevant events from the past. The time frame covers approximately twenty months: Tilly returns to Dungatar in the second half of 1950, just as the football season is winding to a close, and she leaves in March, 1952. This narrative is divided into four sections entitled Gingham, Shantung, Felt and Brocade. While these have an obvious connection to the dressmaking motif, more importantly, the headings correlate to the different stages in Tilly's emotional and creative journey, figuratively reflecting her relationship with the town.

Part I deals with Tilly's arrival in Dungatar. Gingham is an inexpensive, serviceable cotton that can be used for many purposes. It embodies the utilitarian, no-frills sartorial approach of the majority of townspeople. Gingham's very adaptability – it can be used for anything from grain bags to house dresses – suggests that fashion, as such, does not have any particular currency in the town.

In Part II, Tilly introduces couture to the women of Dungatar. Shantung is a vibrant, textured silk, used explicitly for more glamorous designs, signifying the way in which Tilly's creativity enriches their lives. Not only does she make beautiful clothes, but she also tries to explain style and how it can differ from fashion; encouraging the women to choose designs that flatter their body shape, and demonstrating the importance of accessories to complete the image.

Felt is a heavy, dense fabric, made by boiling wool fibres, which is reserved for plain designs. Part III is bookended by the deaths of Teddy and Molly, during which time the town's enmity towards the Dunnages hardens. Tilly no longer sews; instead her creativity is swallowed by grief as she suffers through a distressing period of mourning and alienation.

Brocade is opulent and decorative. In Part IV, Tilly resumes her dressmaking and is restored to tentative favour in the town. When the Social Club commissions baroque costumes for their forthcoming production of *Macbeth*, the bizarre designs afford Tilly the opportunity to mock their pretensions.

Language

Ham's prose is dry and incisive, oscillating swiftly between scathing observational humour and bleak calamity. She has a finely tuned sense of the absurd, and her use of figurative language to portray Dungatar and its characters is memorable. As Tilly surveys the town, she sees the 'green eye of the oval' looking up at her, 'the cars around its edge like lashes' (p.12), confirming the central place football holds in the lives of these people. On a fine day, the low clouds sit 'like lemon butter on toast' (p.77). The residents are described with merciless precision. Crippled by Parkinson's, Mr Almanac is a 'mumbling question mark, forever face-down' (p.24); prior to his sobriety, Fred Bundle had been 'alcohol-pickled' (p.21). When Trudy is restrained by the doctor, she drops to the footpath 'to lie like a discarded cardigan' (p.285), an image that simultaneously conveys her vulnerability and her irrelevance.

The names of many of the residents are puns, reflecting their key characteristics. For example, Evan Pettyman is a small-minded, pompous hypocrite. Beula Harridene is a literal harridan, a spiteful gossip eaten up by hate for the world. Ruth and Prudence Dimm hold responsible positions in the town, but their stupidity and negligence have grim repercussions. By condoning the bullying that Tilly endures, Prudence contributes indirectly to Stewart Pettyman's death, while Ruth's failure to pay for the residents' house insurance means that they are left with nothing after fire destroys the town.

The language of these characters is informed by the 1950s country setting, drawing heavily on the vernacular. Teddy tells Tilly laconically that she's 'not a bad sort of a sheila' (p.175) and one of the young McSwineys accuses a grumpy Beula of having 'shit on [her] liver' (p.50). These idioms contribute to the sense of time and place, as well as delineating character.

Images of light and dark run through the novel. Tilly's essential goodness is represented by the light that often surrounds her. At the races, she is described as 'a luminous statue' (p.108), while, when she sets the blaze that will purge Dungatar, she is surrounded by a dazzling 'halo' of light (p.286). On the other hand, the first view of the town is a 'dark blot' on the horizon (p.1).

Intertextuality in *The Dressmaker*

Intertextuality is a feature of the novel: other well-known texts are referenced throughout. These allusions – usually quotes by the widely read protagonist – link back to the characters or the themes, providing an artful commentary on the interaction taking place. In particular, the Shakespeare plays *Macbeth* and *As You Like It* are cited.

The shadow and example of *Macbeth* hovers over Ham's novel. Like Shakespeare's play, *The Dressmaker* explores issues such as ambition, betrayal, duplicity and reprisal. *Macbeth* is explicitly referenced when the townspeople mount their ill-fated production – a production that fulfils every adverse prophecy made about the 'Scottish play' – and this is the vehicle through which Dungatar self-destructs. Some of the characters in *Macbeth* also find their counterparts in *The Dressmaker*; for example, Trudy's ambition is Lady Macbeth–like in scale and, similarly, she falls victim to that ambition.

Conversely, an oblique parallel is set up between Tilly and the Shakespearean heroine Rosalind, from *As You Like It*. Both are bold, resourceful women who challenge the prevailing stereotypes by refusing to accept the fate that has been mapped out for them. Banished by her uncle, Rosalind flees to the safety of the Forest of Arden, disguised as a boy. Like Rosalind, Tilly is familiar with the pain of banishment and she, too, is playing a part. Aware of the protective camouflage she presents to the world, she warns Teddy not to take her at face value.

Significance of the title

The book's epigraph – the quotation from CF Forbes at the beginning of *The Dressmaker* – highlights the power of clothes, saying that being well-dressed imparts such a sense of 'inward tranquillity' that it transcends even religion. By implication, power is conferred on Tilly for being able to create beautiful clothes. When she first arrives, Tilly announces to Sergeant Farrat that she is 'a seamstress and dressmaker' (p.8) – this is how she defines herself. Her profession becomes the conduit into the insular world of the Dungatar community, the only avenue through which the local women are prepared to connect with her.

The significance of Tilly's original name, Myrtle, is worth noting. The myrtle is a fragrant evergreen shrub with white flowers, native to Europe and North Africa. It was sacred to Demeter, goddess of fertility and the harvest, and Aphrodite, goddess of love. As such, it became a symbol of love and maternity. Though Tilly has been robbed of both, she is presented as a character who deserves love and should remain open to the possibility.

Narrative point of view

The Dressmaker is written in the third person, with an omniscient narrator. This narrative perspective allows Ham to cast an uncompromising eye over her characters, presenting their behaviour in such a way that leaves no doubt as to their faults and foibles.

Events are also presented from the viewpoint of a particular individual, shifting this 'limited' perspective from one character to another. For example, Molly does not initially recognise her daughter, but realises that she will 'have to be crafty, employ stubborn resistance and subtle violence against this stronger woman who was determined to stay' (p.34). In general, though, it is the protagonist's point of view that is given. Presenting events from Tilly's perspective builds empathy and invites a degree of complicity from the reader. At the same time, Tilly's voice is a muted one. She is a guarded character, and she discloses little about her feelings or her history. Information regarding her time in Europe emerges incrementally – some of it teased out by Teddy – but there is still much we don't discover. Hence, Tilly remains an elusive character.

CHAPTER-BY-CHAPTER ANALYSIS

Prologue (pp.1–2)

Summary: *Tilly returns home.*

The prologue establishes the context. Dungatar is a small, isolated town in the Victorian wheatbelt. The description of Molly Dunnage's cottage, sitting alone on the top of the hill that overlooks the town, hints at the reclusive nature of its occupant. Like Molly herself, it leans 'provocatively' (p.1) away from its foundations, but is anchored to the chimney by a thick wisteria. Scandal has dogged Molly; hence The Hill casts a 'shadow' over the town (p.1). Yet it is also 'a shaky beacon in a vast, black sea' (p.1), suggesting it is the one fragile point of comfort in a dark, unwelcoming setting.

Tilly's attempts at reaching her mother have been met with unhelpful stonewalling by the 'curt voice' (p.1) at the telephone exchange. Molly is dismissed as old, mad and unable to communicate, alerting readers to the contempt in which she is held by the locals.

PART I: GINGHAM

Chapter One (pp.5–12)

Summary: *Tilly is reunited with her mother.*

First impressions of Tilly are of a stylish, self-sufficient young woman. Watching her arrival, the curious Sergeant Farrat admires the cut and quality of her clothes, and homes in on her Singer sewing machine. This machine, symbolising possibility and creativity, is one of the enduring motifs in the text. Tilly's feelings upon returning to Dungatar are clearly conflicted; Farrat's offer to take her 'the long way home' (p.7) reignites memories of an unhappy childhood and hardens the knot in Tilly's stomach.

She faces a daunting, and thankless, task. The house is filthy and her mother, seemingly, does not know her. Molly is in a pitiful state; she has lived alone in poverty and neglect for years, her language is maniacal and she suffers delusions. Tilly holds the town directly responsible: 'This is what they've done to you' (p.9).

Key vocabulary

Night cart man: before the advent of sewerage systems, the night cart man collected and disposed of the town's excrement, which was deposited in portable, purpose-built cans.

Chapter Two (pp.13–27)

Summary: *Saturday morning in the town; Dungatar wins the football final.*

Chapter Two introduces many of the individuals who make up the town's collective character. Dungatar is a microcosm, a miniature reflection of the wider world beyond its boundaries, where all aspects of human behaviour are on display. For example, industry is represented by the Pratts, snobbery by the Beaumonts, spite by Beula Harridene, tolerance by Sergeant Farrat, infidelity by Faith O'Brien, cruelty by Mr Almanac and good fellowship by the Bundles.

On the surface, Dungatar appears to be an agnostic culture. There is no church and Sergeant Farrat is the closest the town has to a minister. Football is, in fact, the town's religion. The local team inspires a fierce, parochial loyalty; arriving at the pub after their latest win, the victors are embraced affectionately by the publican's wife as 'My boys!' (p.26).

Chapter Three (pp.28–33)

Summary: *Tilly meets Teddy McSwiney.*

The McSwineys are a close-knit family who lead a shambolic but honest existence. Having watched Tilly's arrival with great interest, Teddy McSwiney introduces himself at the earliest opportunity. Generous and practical, his offer of a wheelchair prompts Tilly to wonder, ironically, 'if the rest of the town would be as friendly' (p.32). However, Teddy's teasing comment, 'I'm the one should be frightened of you' (p.32), foreshadows the tragedy that lies ahead for them both.

The wheelchair symbolises Molly's dependence, yet it will also enable her to leave the house and reconnect with the town.

Q What does Molly's comment that 'you can't keep anything secret here' (p.33) reveal about Dungatar?

Chapter Four (pp.34–41)

Summary: *Tilly takes her mother into town.*

The Dunnages' presence in the town is regarded as an affront, prompting a judgemental frenzy. Those watching the pair's progress fall back on the old pejorative stereotypes: Tilly is the 'illegitimate girl' and Molly, the 'loose woman and hag' (p.39).

Nevertheless, there are exceptions. Irma Almanac, a gentle woman who has been covertly sending food to Molly for years, compliments Tilly on her bravery in returning home to look after her mother. Like Molly, Irma has suffered abuse. Her troubles have been solved by natural attrition: advanced Parkinson's disease has reduced her husband to 'a stiff and shuffling old man' (p.41), unable to inflict any further injury on his wife.

Key point

Tilly's return reignites the town's animosity. Most of the residents resent her presence and are still prepared to judge her harshly for events in the past.

Q Does Tilly empower herself by returning to Dungatar, or is she undermined by the decision?

Chapter Five (pp.42–51)

Summary: *Beula makes a complaint against the McSwineys.*

In this chapter, Beula Harridene's malice is set in opposition to Sergeant Farrat's goodwill. Beula represents the worst that Dungatar has to offer; she spies on her neighbours and sees evil everywhere. Sergeant Farrat indulges her up to a point – his theory is that Beula is starving because 'her bite is inefficient' (p.45) and she is 'therefore vicious, malnourished and mad' (p.46). Beyond that, he refuses to accommodate her, preferring to treat people – including the McSwineys – with compassion and civility.

Chapter Six (pp.52–60)

Summary: *Gertrude sets her sights on William Beaumont; Tilly remembers her schooldays; Evan Pettyman ministers to Marigold.*

Gertrude may be plain and unsophisticated, but she dares to imagine what her parents cannot – a future where she is married to William Beaumont. The Beaumonts see themselves as better than everyone else in the community; however, they trade on their social standing and don't pay their bills.

Dungatar's ugly underbelly is exposed through Tilly's painful memories of being bullied at school – by both the teacher and the children – and Councillor Pettyman's unscrupulous treatment of his wife. Prudence Dimm's viciousness and Pettyman's exploitation of women are two of the factors that have made Tilly's life so unbearable in the past.

Q What do Gertrude and the Beaumonts have in common?

Chapter Seven (pp.61–8)

Summary: *Dungatar wins the grand final.*

Football is the key element that unites this eclectic community. After Dungatar's football team wins the final against Winyerp, the watching crowd erupts with 'lust, revenge, joy, hate and elation' (p.66). The entire town celebrates with riotous enthusiasm at the pub: 'No team was ever happier, no town ever noisier' (p.66). Teddy is the hero of the hour, having dribbled the ball through for the winning point at the last minute, cementing his place as Dungatar's favourite son.

At the same time, Teddy's interest in the 'new sheila' (p.63) has been noted, and his protectiveness towards her is also unambiguously brought home to his friends. Teddy's love for Tilly will create a conflict of interest that cannot be easily reconciled with his relationship with the town, forcing him to make a choice between the two.

Q What is Septimus Crescant suggesting when he talks about 'the end' and says 'of course there's The Hill' (p.68)?

Chapter Eight (pp.69–83)

Summary: *Tilly's tea-chest arrives; Teddy asks her to the dance; Tilly makes Irma some special cakes.*

Trains represent Dungatar's connection to the outside world. Tilly's tea-chest (packing case) hints at travels and experiences far beyond the imagination of any of the townspeople. Her worldliness is a constant challenge to their insularity. Tilly's knowledge of herbal remedies is more efficacious than Mr Almanac's conventional treatments, and her 'special cakes' (likely containing cannabis, p.77) alleviate his wife's arthritic pain for the first time in years.

Teddy finds Tilly exotic and interesting, and his campaign to win her affections is 'indefatigable' (p.81). He brings her fresh fish and garden produce, in addition to cooking for her. Molly is not so mad that she doesn't recognise Teddy's worth; when Tilly refuses to go to the footballers' dance with him, Molly sulks for two days. The old woman still does not seem to appreciate the loving care that Tilly gives her. When she can't get her own way, she behaves like an unpredictable child, oblivious to consequences.

Q Teddy believes 'girls like her [Tilly] need a bloke like me about' (p74). Why does he think this? Do you agree?

Chapter Nine (pp.84–91)

Summary: *Tilly goes to the dance with Teddy; Gertrude wins William Beaumont.*

The evening is a memorable one for several who attend. After sweeping the inexperienced William off his feet, Gertrude uses her sexuality as a lure and successfully ensnares her quarry.

Teddy also gets his wish and has Tilly on his arm as his partner. However, despite his popularity, the young couple are ostracised all night. For Tilly, the experience reinforces her sense that she is 'unworthy' (p.89): 'She knew it was a mistake, it was too soon, too bold' (p.88). She admits to herself that she is used to forgetting her so-called guilt, only to be reminded in cruel, gratuitous ways by the people of Dungatar.

Key point

Teddy is dismissive of the town's attitude – 'They'll just have to get used to you' (p.91) – but Tilly concludes that the reverse is true. The town will not change and she is the one who will need to adapt.

Q Why does Tilly go to the dance?

PART II: SHANTUNG

Chapter Ten (pp.95–100)

Summary: *The dance is discussed by the locals.*

Gossip, fuelled primarily by Beula Harridene, is one of Dungatar's primary pastimes. Tilly's appearance at the dance and, in particular, the eye-catching green dress, has set tongues wagging. Typically, Beula says 'everybody was speechless with disgust' (p.98). Again, Tilly's sophistication is thrown into sharp relief: her sartorial style has been honed by years of working at the great couture houses of Europe, and is a world away from the outdated fashions of the local women.

Chapter Eleven (pp.101–9)

Summary: *Tilly goes to the races.*

The races are a further opportunity for Tilly to promote her dressmaking skills. This time she wears a glamorous dress of amethyst shantung that shimmers as she walks, catching the light, as well as the attention of the other racegoers: 'She looked like some-one out of a movie and the air around her seemed different' (p.107). The Dungatar women, dowdy in their 'sensible floral cotton button-throughs with box cluster pleat skirts' (p.106), can only stare in envy.

Pragmatically, Gertrude Pratt homes in on the fact that Tilly is a dressmaker. Preoccupied with the wedding that she hopes is forthcoming, Gertrude's desire to be a beautiful bride overrides any scruples she may have about Tilly herself.

Q What does the phrase 'marry down' (p.109) mean? What does this reveal about societal values in country Australia in the 1950s?

Chapter Twelve (pp.110–15)

Summary: *Tilly makes Gertrude's wedding dress.*

Tilly successfully appeals to Gertrude's vanity when she steers her away from her original choice of wedding gown, which would have done little to minimise her worst features: 'Oh no … we can do much better than that' (p.111). Both Tilly and Gertrude will eventually benefit from this transaction.

Although Tilly is coming to rely on Teddy more and more – not least in relation to managing Molly's moods and tantrums – there are still times when she is unwilling, or unable, to let down her emotional guard. Her enigmatic refusal to go to the McSwineys' for a Christmas drink– 'That would break my heart' (p.115) – is one such occasion.

Q Why is Molly so hostile to her own daughter?

Chapter Thirteen (pp.116–25)

Summary: *Gertrude marries William; Tilly remembers Stewart Pettyman.*

Gertrude's dazzling entrance at her wedding surprises and delights her new husband, diffusing any qualms he may have about the suitability of the marriage. Thanks to Tilly, Gertrude is a lovely bride, 'curvy and succulent' (p.118). The women in the congregation note that the dressmaker is 'an absolute wizard with fabric and scissors' (p.119) though, unfortunately, they are not able to find out her name.

Snubbed by the wedding party, Tilly's thoughts turn to her unhappy schooldays. Taunted by her classmates, threatened and physically assaulted by Stewart Pettyman, her dominant memories are of fear and exclusion.

Chapter Fourteen (pp.126–33)

Summary: *Tilly gets some customers.*

The freight trains that rumble into Dungatar to empty the silos and transport the grain are part of the cycle of the farming calendar that defines towns such as this. The activity attracts the attention of the local children who play around the looming silo and the grain trucks – just as the young Teddy McSwiney and his friends did in the past. Some of these trucks are filled with wheat, some with sorghum. The scene, seemingly benign, foreshadows Teddy's accident.

Word of Tilly's dressmaking has spread through the town in the wake of the Beaumont wedding. One by one, the ladies of Dungatar climb The Hill with their various requests, which run the gamut from modest mending to the making of school uniforms. Nancy Pickett, more daringly, commissions a trouser suit.

Key vocabulary

Cristóbal Balenciaga: a Spanish designer who opened his own fashion house in Paris in 1937 and became one of the most successful postwar couturiers.

Sorghum: a widely cultivated grain that can be used for human or animal consumption, or to make ethanol. In Australia, it is used primarily as livestock feed.

Madeleine Vionnet: an influential French fashion designer of the early twentieth century who was particularly known for the bias cut (cutting cloth diagonally to the fabric's grain, which helps it to cling to the body).

Q Why is Molly so preoccupied with the possum?

Chapter Fifteen (pp.134–44)

Summary: *The Beaumonts return to Dungatar, accompanied by Lesley Muncan; the Social Club is launched; Tilly's business takes off.*

Throughout the text, the experiences and choices of Tilly and Gertrude Pratt are thrown into sharp relief. Like Tilly, Gertrude has reinvented herself. However, whereas Tilly's new identity is a legitimate attempt to escape her painful past and is accompanied by a professional life of creativity and purpose, Gertrude's switch to 'Trudy' is simply an affectation. When she returns from her shopping spree in Melbourne, intending to impress, she and Elsbeth are miffed to discover how well-dressed Dungatar has suddenly become. It is generally conceded that 'Tilly can do magic' (p.134).

Tilly's dressmaking skills play into the women's aspirations of social betterment. Genuine self-expression is less important than looking, and therefore feeling, superior to one's neighbours, 'especially Elsbeth' (p.142). Tilly notes that, taking their cue from 'Trudy', the members of the newly established Social Club have acquired posh accents overnight, 'an enunciated Dungatar interpretation of queenly English' (p.142). Elsbeth's initial resistance to her son's choice of bride is weakened by the discovery that she and Trudy have much in common, and the welcome news of a pregnancy.

Chapter Sixteen (pp.145–58)

Summary: *The Social Club holds a fundraising day at Windswept Crest.*

Windswept Crest's nickname of 'Fart Hill' (p.139) reflects the town's secret contempt for Elsbeth Beaumont. At the fundraising day, those invited are under no illusion that they are effectively raising money for the Beaumont family's coffers and to pay for the proposed improvements to the property. While the guests eschew croquet, opting instead for football, Trudy counts the money. Privately, Muriel Pratt deplores the fact that, since her daughter's marriage, Trudy has absorbed Elsbeth's snobbery and 'turned into the sort of person I moved here to avoid' (p.150).

With Trudy's arrival, William's sister Mona finds herself ostracised. Desperate for affirmation and companionship, she gravitates towards Lesley Muncan, who is equally friendless and the only one kind to her.

Q Comment on the way in which Teddy manages Molly. What does it show about him?

Chapter Seventeen (pp.159–73)

Summary: *Mona and Lesley get married; a stranger visits Dungatar; preparations are underway for the ball.*

Elsbeth Beaumont sees her daughter as a problem to be solved, and cynically exploits Mona's indiscretion with Lesley to rush her into marriage. Although the discovery of her new husband's impotence is a shock and a disappointment, Mona is persuaded by Lesley that a marriage can also be founded on friendship and compromise: 'we'll do the best we can together' (p.173).

The stranger's arrival in Dungatar puts Tilly's accomplishments into perspective. Observing that the local women dress 'astonishingly well' (p.164), the traveller is so impressed that she seeks Tilly out to order some designs and offer her a job in Melbourne.

Tilly denies that she is wasting her talents in Dungatar and, certainly, the extensive preparations for the ball place even more demands on her time. Tilly designs for each individual's body shape, maximising their attributes and minimising their faults. She takes a holistic approach, teaching her clients that true style goes beyond merely wearing the clothes. Rather, it is a synthesis of many elements, which include grooming, deportment and the right accessories. The women of Dungatar embrace the opportunity to assume more glamorous personas, acting out their fantasies – 'Faith's a red sequins kind of woman' (p.171) – and reinventing themselves as stylish and desirable. Nevertheless, recognising the town's limitations, Sergeant Farrat is the only one who truly appreciates Tilly's efforts.

Key point

Throughout *The Dressmaker*, fashion is presented as a metaphor for change. Tilly's designs offer her clients a unique opportunity to express and transform themselves in previously unimagined ways.

Chapter Eighteen (pp.174–87)

Summary: *Tilly is shunned at the ball; she and Teddy declare their love; Teddy dies in an accident.*

Quoting from Rosalind in *As You like It*, Tilly tries to warn Teddy off: 'I pray you, do not fall in love with me, For I am falser than vows made in wine' (p.176). It is not the first time that Tilly has hidden behind an evasive quotation, but it is the most explicit. In Shakespeare's play, Rosalind, cross-dressing as a boy, tells Phebe not to fall in love with him (her). Like Tilly, Rosalind is escaping from her past and runs into unsolicited romantic complications. Racked with self-doubt, Tilly is implying to Teddy that she is not what he thinks, and that any relationship between them would be a mistake.

Equally, Tilly knows that she is running a risk in going to the ball, but she finally acquiesces because she trusts Teddy: 'He was her good friend and he was her ally' (p.177). Her fabulous dress, a customised adaptation of one of Dior's most celebrated gowns, prompts her mother's wry comment that 'girls who wear dresses like that don't warrant honourable intentions' (p.178). In retrospect, Molly's joke takes on an ominous edge.

Although the occasion becomes a spectacular fashion parade, a tribute to Tilly's creativity and skill, Dungatar's hostility is again brought home to her when she is decisively rejected by those present. Nobody wants her on their table; Evan Pettyman and Beula Harridene are openly abusive. The cruelty with which Tilly is treated demonstrates that nothing has really changed. Despite the glamorous image Tilly has crafted for them, the majority of the Dungatar women remain mean-spirited and small-minded, resistant to self-improvement on any meaningful level.

When, in a dark twist of fate, the future that Teddy plans is shattered by his unexpected death, Tilly's belief that she carries 'evil' inside her (p.184) becomes a self-fulfilling prophecy.

Key vocabulary

Dior: Christian Dior, one of the most influential French fashion designers of the postwar period.

Q Tilly's brilliant magenta dress subliminally suggests a 'scarlet woman'. Is she challenging this stereotype or accommodating it?

Q How would you describe the influence that Tilly has had on these women?

PART III: FELT

Chapter Nineteen (pp.191–200)

Summary: *The town mourns Teddy McSwiney.*

The tone of this chapter is elegiac as Dungatar comes to terms with the loss of their 'hero' (p.194). At the 'severe, cruel burial' (p.196), the congregation is in no mood to absorb Sergeant Farrat's message of love and forgiveness.

Edward McSwiney decides to take his family away from Dungatar and, in an act that foreshadows Tilly's incineration of the town, burns the caravans and railway carriages that have been their home.

The McSwineys' loss mirrors that of other bereaved parents in the town. With typical empathy, Farrat recognises how grief distorts perspective, even causing madness. Molly Dunnage and Marigold Pettyman, for example, have drowned 'in the grief and disgust that hung like cobwebs' everywhere they look (p.194). To an extent, the same thing happens to Dungatar. In their 'stunned rage and wretchedness' (p.198), the townspeople forget the fragile truce that has been established with the Dunnages and single out Tilly as their scapegoat. Full of despair and self-loathing, and haunted by memories of Stewart Pettyman, Tilly absorbs the town's blame.

Q Sergeant Farrat asserts that 'tragedy includes everyone' and that everyone in the town is '*different*, yet included' (p.196). Do you agree? Look at *both* parts of his claim.

Chapter Twenty (pp.201–2)

Summary: *The Dunnages are persecuted by the townspeople.*

The physical isolation of the Dunnages' house on top of The Hill reinforces their alienation from the town. Not all of Dungatar's residents are as malevolent as Beula Harridene or Evan Pettyman, yet the town is united in its determination to believe the worst of Tilly, relentlessly targeting her and her mother. As she nurses her own grief, Tilly's bitterness grows.

Chapter Twenty One (pp.203–9)

Summary: *Una Pleasance arrives in Dungatar.*

Sponsored by the Social Club, Una Pleasance has arrived to open her own dressmaking establishment, *Le Salon*, and, true to form, Evan Pettyman targets the 'new girl in town' (p.204) with practised ease. Abandoned by the townspeople, Tilly's only work comes from her sole remaining friend, Sergeant Farrat; his green matador costume is a subliminal homage to the Spanish heritage of Tilly's old teacher, Cristóbal Balenciaga.

Key vocabulary

Balmain: Pierre Balmain, a French fashion designer.

Chapter Twenty Two (pp.210–14)

Summary: *Una opens* Le Salon*; Gertrude has her baby.*

Una's dressmaking is of a very different calibre from Tilly's; her designs are pedestrian and the standard of her work mediocre. The opening of the new business, temporarily located at the Pettymans', degenerates into farce when Trudy unexpectedly goes into labour. Avid for gossip, Beula is quick to seize on the fact that Trudy has only been married eight months. By the time Evan returns home, he finds his house in chaos and his neurotic wife prostrate in bed.

Key vocabulary

Rockmans: a women's clothing store in Melbourne catering to the cheaper end of the market.

Q What does this chapter reveal about the relationship between Trudy and Elsbeth?

Chapter Twenty Three (pp.215–20)

Summary: *Tilly's skills are sought by the women of Winyerp.*

Tilly's garden is another manifestation of her creativity. Lush and beautiful, its stunning colours reflect the variety of her designs. As the McSwineys previously discovered, the tip – on face value the dumping ground for the town's discarded refuse – can provide unexpected benefits. Although 'the stink of burning rubbish' (p.215) mingles with the garden's perfume, its ash is good for the soil; ironically, the residents' attempt to smoke the Dunnages out has enabled Tilly's plants to flourish.

Tilly's namesake plant, the myrtle, features prominently, its 'shiny green leaves and bright white flowers' (p.215) threading their way through the other plants and creeping across the veranda. The garden highlights Tilly's resilience and represents healing. After a period of mourning and inactivity, she resumes her dressmaking, this time for an appreciative clientele from Winyerp.

In suggesting the drama competition to Mrs Flynt from Winyerp, Tilly is able to use Elsbeth Beaumont's one-upmanship against her. As Tilly presciently observes, plays 'bring out the best and worst in people' (p.219).

Q Why does Molly decorate her wheelchair?

Chapter Twenty Four (pp.221–7)

Summary: *Evan and Una start an affair; an eisteddfod is planned.*

Tilly's mischievous suggestion of a play has taken root. Representatives from the Winyerp and Itheca Drama Club, looking like 'a group of European aristocrats' wives who had somehow lost their way' (p.225), invite Dungatar to participate in a drama eisteddfod. As Una's inadequacies as a dressmaker have become glaringly obvious, the women of Dungatar have a change of heart. In the interests of expediency, the past is conveniently forgotten and Tilly is reclaimed as one of their own.

Q Why is Marigold so obsessed with cleaning?

Chapter Twenty Five (pp.228–9)

Summary: *Una returns to Melbourne.*

The lonely departure of 'Miss Unpleasant' (p.228) – as Faith has christened her – from Dungatar is in marked contrast to the fanfare that accompanied her arrival. Nevertheless, Una's absence does not dampen Evan's enthusiasm. Drugged and preoccupied, Marigold has a shockingly distorted perception of her husband – 'You're so important, Evan' (p.229). The calculated indifference he feels towards his wife is evident when he masturbates in front of his mistress' photograph.

Chapter Twenty Six (pp.230–6)

Summary: *Tilly is reconciled with her mother; Molly suffers a stroke and dies.*

Molly's inexplicable dream of her grandson introduces an element of magical realism into the novel. Previously ignorant of Pablo's existence, Molly's dream provides the trigger that finally enables her to connect with her daughter in a meaningful way, and she and Tilly share their stories. Brought together by their mutual loss, mother and daughter can only comfort each other and mourn the lost years, before they are parted again by Molly's death.

Though she has options in Melbourne, Tilly decides that first she has accounts to settle in Dungatar: 'It seems only fair don't you think?' (p.236).

Key point

Molly's death is a turning point for Tilly. She resolves to take revenge on the people of Dungatar for all their sins of omission and deliberate cruelty. The pain that she and Molly have endured will be the driving force – her 'catalyst' and 'propeller' – for change (p.236).

Q Are there any positives to come out of Molly's death?

PART IV: BROCADE

Chapter Twenty Seven (pp.239–52)

Summary: *Tilly and Sergeant Farrat bury Molly; Beula is badly injured; Mr Almanac drowns; Tilly agrees to make the costumes for* Macbeth.

This chapter commences with Molly's funeral – a sad and lonely affair attended only by Tilly and the sergeant – but afterwards, for the first time since her arrival in Dungatar, the wheels of justice start to turn in Tilly's favour.

Beula Harridene and Mr Almanac are both punished for their vindictiveness towards Molly. Beula's spying puts her in the wrong place at the wrong time and, after being struck by an airborne radiogram, her refusal to seek immediate help makes the injury worse. Mr Almanac meets his own fitting end when he stumbles into the creek while his wife dozes. Standing by her mother's grave, Tilly gleefully remembers that 'sometimes things just don't *seem* fair' (p.248).

The Social Club's choice to stage *Macbeth* is apposite, given that Trudy and her acolytes are guilty of both ambition and the figurative murder of the Dunnages. Approached by the women to sew their costumes, Tilly is able to exploit Trudy's vanity and ignorance by encouraging her choice of the flamboyant baroque designs. These costumes are not only contextually unsuitable for *Macbeth*, they will also prove very costly in the long run.

Key vocabulary

Radiogram: a combined radio and record player; in the 1950s it would have been a substantial piece of furniture.

Q Does Tilly choose wisely when she agrees to make the costumes?

Chapter Twenty Eight (pp.253–9)

Summary: *Tilly visits Marigold to tell her the truth; Marigold kills Evan and then attempts to take her own life.*

Dungatar's streak of accidents and deaths continues when Marigold, emboldened by Tilly, takes matters into her own hands and effects a ruthless revenge on her philandering husband. The story of Molly's seduction resonates with Marigold because it is effectively her own story too. Freed from the toxic confusion caused by drugs, Marigold is able to see the actions of her husband – and son – clearly. While the truth hardens her resolve, it also leads to despair. The knowledge that Evan has manipulated and betrayed her, and that Stewart, whom she idolised, was in reality a nasty little bully, leaves Marigold with nothing.

Chapter Twenty Nine (pp.260–6)

Summary: *The district inspector arrives to investigate the proliferation of deaths in Dungatar.*

Dreams are important in *The Dressmaker*, taking on a value that goes beyond a haphazard expression of the subconscious. Tilly's dream of her lost loved ones is a powerful indicator of her readiness to take control over the forces that have threated to overwhelm her. Although the citizens of Dungatar crawl 'up The Hill in the dark, armed with firewood and flames, stakes and chains', Tilly merely smiles down at them from her veranda and 'they turned and fled' (p.261).

Fate continues to play into her hands. Far from posing a threat, the district inspector is discovered to be a fool, whose inflated sense of self-importance precludes any real investigative talent. To Sergeant Farrat's mortification, his uninvited guest is also extremely uncouth, with 'slovenly habits and very bad manners' (p.262). After the inspector's visit, Tilly decides that she can proceed with her agenda, as 'there's nothing to be afraid of' (p.265).

Chapter Thirty (pp.267–78)

Summary: *Rehearsals get underway; Tilly finishes the costumes.*

The curse of the 'Scottish play' becomes a self-fulfilling prophecy when, living up to its traditional reputation as unlucky, things start to go wrong with *Macbeth* from the outset. Director and producer are at constant loggerheads, the actors are out of their depth, and funding for the production becomes an issue. Tilly watches the chaos with quiet satisfaction.

Key point

The baroque costumes – heavy, uncomfortable and completely inappropriate – are a symbol of Dungatar's false values. The townspeople become complicit in their own downfall; the critical decision to prioritise the costumes over their insurance premiums will destroy their futures.

Q Is the play only bringing out the worst in the townspeople?

Chapter Thirty One (pp.279–82)

Summary: *Rehearsals become more stressful.*

As rehearsals start to implode, the browbeaten cast threatens to rebel against Trudy's maniacal authority. Like Lady Macbeth, Trudy is a casualty of her own ambition. She becomes increasingly unstable, finally having a breakdown just as the hoped-for prize is within reach.

Chapter Thirty Two (pp.283–93)

Summary: *After setting her house on fire, Tilly leaves town; the production is a disaster.*

Trudy's mind is *'full of scorpions'* (p.285) and she is deemed unfit to continue. Her breakdown is an ominous portent, the bus refusing to start is another. Predictably, this is one production that does not come together on the day. When the dreadful performance is terminated prematurely after Act 1, Dungatar's humiliation is complete.

As the townspeople struggle through the play, Tilly makes her own preparations. Like an avenging angel, she is ruthless and methodical, doing everything to ensure that her house will burn rapidly and the fire will spread. Sergeant Farrat, running late for the eisteddfod, can do nothing.

Q How does Malcolm's line from *Macbeth* – 'The night is long that never finds the day' (p.287) – relate to Tilly?

Chapter Thirty Three (pp.294–6)

Summary: *The residents of Dungatar return to find their town destroyed.*

Although Tilly's work wins the cup for 'Best Costume', this is no compensation for the devastation that greets the actors when they return home. With the exception of Windswept Crest, Dungatar has been razed to the ground. The people who made the Dunnages' lives such a misery are left 'homeless and heartbroken' (p.295) and, in a perverse twist of fate, dependent on Elsbeth Beaumont's goodwill.

Key point

Traditionally, fire is seen as a cleansing agent that purges infection and disease, a symbol of rebirth. Tilly has provided the town with a chance to redeem itself by rising from the ashes with a clean slate and a fresh moral perspective – whether people choose to avail themselves of the opportunity or not.

Q How do you view Tilly's destruction of the town? Is it out of character?

CHARACTERS & RELATIONSHIPS

Myrtle (Tilly) Dunnage

Key quotes

'My name is Tilly … Everyone will know soon enough.' (p.7)

'Tell me, why did a beautiful and clever girl like you come back here?' (Irma, p.78)

'Bitterness rested on Tilly's soul and wore itself on her face.' (p.202)

Tilly Dunnage is a remarkable young woman. A disadvantaged background and a childhood marred by tragedy have not prevented her from achieving success. She empowers herself by travelling to Europe and forging an independent career, eventually setting up her own shop in Paris (p.231). Defying convention, Tilly lives with her English lover, Ormond, and – like her mother before her – has a child out of wedlock. However, this child is conceived in love and born into a welcoming context.

After her life in Paris implodes, Tilly returns to Dungatar to nurse her ailing mother, thinking that she can be of use to Molly. Unfortunately, the relationship is fraught. Far from appreciating her daughter's selflessness, the old woman is difficult, contrary and sometimes violent. In response to her mother's tantrums, Tilly is stoic and philosophical.

The general consensus in Dungatar is that Tilly has a 'nerve' (p.35). Molly Dunnage's 'bastard girl' (p.64) is resented by the locals, whose perception of her is fuelled by vicious gossip and a distorted understanding of the past. Tilly stands out in the small town like an exotic bird of paradise and, at first, her arresting sartorial style provokes hostility in a community suspicious of difference. The bright rainbow colours she favours – green, purple, crimson – are in marked contrast to the drab attire of the local women. Tilly has been trained by the great couturiers in Paris – Balmain, Balenciaga and Dior – all of whom recognised her exceptional talent. She has the imagination to see the potential in a piece of discounted georgette and turn it into the stunning green gown that she wears to the dance. Tilly's designs are impossible to ignore and the women of Dungatar cannot resist utilising her talents to improve their own wardrobes.

Tilly is happiest when she is creating. In spite of the limitations and shortcomings of her 'inglorious' clientele (p.128), she welcomes having a business to run again. Nevertheless, she is reminded on several occasions, and with brutal clarity, that she is being used by the townspeople. Sergeant Farrat is one of the few who truly values her presence in Dungatar, saying, 'Without Tilly's tolerance and generosity, her patience and skills, our lives – mine especially – would not have been enriched' (p.239).

Tilly's vulnerability is evident to Farrat from the outset. Scarred by loss and burdened by guilt, she blames herself, erroneously, for the tragic deaths of Stewart Pettyman and her baby son. Rather than seeing herself as the victim she truly is, Tilly judges herself as harshly as her home town and her lover have done. As such, she initially perceives Teddy as someone she will damage. Gradually she responds to his love and unshakable conviction that they belong together. However, every time Tilly rebuilds her life, tragedy strikes, reinforcing her sense of unworthiness and reducing her ability to see events objectively. After Teddy's accident, her exhausted mind races with hatred for both herself and the unforgiving townspeople, and she prays 'to a God she didn't believe in to come and take her away' (p.199).

As long as her mother is alive, Tilly feels that her only option is to remain in Dungatar as penance. However, Molly's unhappy death hardens Tilly's resolve and frees her to act. In setting the fire and ensuring its spread, she literally destroys her past. Tilly's actions are ruthless in the extreme; her lack of mercy, in fact, mirrors the town's own behaviour. Wearing a new travelling outfit, she turns her back on her home town without compunction and leaves for a better life in Melbourne.

Key point

Tilly's personal journey has encompassed loss and despair. However, the conclusion of the novel depicts a strong, resilient woman who has gained agency and empowerment by reasserting control over her future.

Teddy McSwiney

Key quotes

'Teddy was Mae's firstborn, her dashing boy – cheeky, quick and canny.' (p.28)

'You'll be safe with Teddy.' (Farrat, p.171)

Like Tilly, Teddy is an outlier. He is the eldest of the prolific McSwiney tribe – a family who live in a collection of disused railway carriages and old caravans beside the tip. His father has the lowly job of night cart man and Teddy would simply be another McSwiney, interchangeable with his many siblings and just as poorly regarded, were it not for the fact that he is 'Dungatar's highly valued full forward' (p.28). As captain and an integral member of the football team, Teddy enjoys the admiration and esteem of the whole town. He is as entrepreneurial off the field as he is courageous on it, and his energy and generosity are deployed in organising card games, Saturday-night dances and fundraising raffles – all of which further endear him to the locals. The general view is that 'Teddy McSwiney could sell a sailor sea-water' (p.28).

Cheerful and good-humoured, Teddy is the perfect foil for Tilly, the light to her darkness. His feelings for her are immediate. She is worldly and sophisticated, different from anyone else he has known. A supreme optimist and used to charming women, Teddy is undeterred by Tilly's aloofness. Nor does he care about her reputation, or Dungatar's obvious disapproval of their relationship. Teddy recognises the loneliness beneath Tilly's independent shell, using guile and persistence to wear down her defences until she starts to rely on him. Believing that she has found 'something golden' (p.192), she agrees to marry him.

However, Teddy's fearlessness is his undoing. Categorically rejecting Tilly's belief that she is 'cursed' (p.195), he dies attempting to prove that 'the might of his love' (p.197) will shield her from further harm. Instead, his tragic death compounds her feelings of guilt and brings the town's hatred down on her head. Grimly, Sergeant Farrat tells the congregation at Teddy's funeral that 'you are not as large as he in heart, nor will you ever be, and that is the sad fact' (p.197). In one perverse respect at least, Teddy's death is like that of Stewart Pettyman: though Tilly stands accused, each of these individuals is responsible for his own fate.

Key point

The people of Dungatar have put Teddy on a pedestal and their emotional investment encourages a misplaced sense of ownership. That this hero-worship is inherently dangerous is evidenced by the town's irrational fury after they lose him.

Molly Dunnage

Key quotes

'Molly Dunnage, mad woman and crone ...' (p.8)

'... hers was a life lived with trouble travelling alongside ...' (Farrat, p.241)

Molly's presence in the town has always been resented; metaphorically, she has lived in the dark, 'a shadow in a sad place' (p.236). She was a sheltered only child, still unmarried at a relatively late age, when she naively succumbed to Evan Pettyman's oily charms. Rejected by her conservative Christian parents when she would not give up her baby, Molly had come to Dungatar for a fresh start, only to be pursued by Pettyman. With no money and an illegitimate child to support, Molly had few defences against Pettyman's relentless harassment and, unwillingly, became his mistress. Later she insists that, without his intervention, 'Myrtle and I could have had some sort of life' (p.194). Pettyman continued to exercise a malign influence on Molly's existence, wielding his power to rob her of her child after his own son's death.

When Tilly first returns to Dungatar, Molly is irrational and resents her daughter's efforts to look after her. If she is crossed, she lashes out in bizarre ways. On one occasion, she dismantles Tilly's sewing machine and hides the parts; on another, she hits Tilly over the head with a poker. Equally, she shows no inclination, or ability, to curb her tongue and can say some vicious, hurtful things. More out of habit than malice, she calls Barney McSwiney a 'spastic' (p.103), though most of her insults are reserved for Tilly.

Molly's initial hostility towards her daughter is the result of a mind clouded by grief and misfortune. Wretched, shunned and prematurely aged, Molly has lived for twenty years separated from her beloved child, with no idea of her whereabouts. By her own admission, she literally goes 'mad with loneliness' (p.232). While the old woman becomes used to Tilly's presence in the house, arguably she does not regain her wits until just before she dies. In between the good and the not-so-good days, the best that Tilly can say is that Molly is 'always entertaining and things come back to her from time to time' (p.146).

Molly's death is cruel and untimely, and the reconciliation with her daughter fleeting. However, Tilly is, at least, offered a glimpse of the woman she has missed. Lucid and purposeful after dreaming of her grandson, Molly is finally able to convey the depths of her love, and the pair grieve together: 'Sorry, so sorry, they said to each other' (p.233).

Sergeant Farrat

Key quotes

'Sergeant Farrat said love was as strong as hate ...' (p.196)

'I'm beyond caring what those people think or say anymore. I'm sure everyone's seen what's on my clothes line over the years ...' (p.241)

Kind, tolerant and perceptive, Horatio Farrat is also an outsider. He is originally from Melbourne, but his attempts to design new uniforms as a young police graduate raised enough disquiet in the minds of his superiors for him to be posted to the isolated town of Dungatar. Sergeant

Farrat's attitude towards law enforcement is fluid. According to Beula Harridene, his 'clock's set wrong' (p.45), but most of the residents appreciate his leniency. Although Farrat loves his adopted home, he is somewhat detached from its concerns – being invested in neither football nor drinking – and set apart by his own unconventional proclivities. In private, he enjoys designing and sewing (female) clothes, which he wears on holiday in Melbourne: 'The outfits didn't necessarily compliment his physique, but they were unique' (p.20). The sergeant is particularly fond of the spring fashion shows at Myer and David Jones.

Farrat's sympathies are equally removed from the mainstream. He befriends Tilly when she returns to Dungatar, recognising her as a kindred creative spirit, and deploring the injustice with which she has been treated by the town. At the same time, the sergeant has a proprietorial concern for 'his flock' (p.201). He is a consistent force for good, whose role is to monitor, listen and encourage the people of Dungatar to show charity. At Teddy's funeral, Farrat condemns the prevailing hatred as dangerous and divisive, preaching love and inclusion instead. He remains Tilly's only ally – 'I knew a bit of needlework would lift your spirits' (p.209) – and provides unwavering support as her mother is dying. In an audacious gesture of solidarity, Farrat even wears one of his own outfits when he accompanies Tilly to Molly's funeral.

Gertrude (Trudy) Pratt

Key quotes

'Our Gert's a handsome, capable girl.' (Muriel, p.16)

'Reckon she might cost a few bob to run, that one.' (Scotty, p.87)

Gertrude, aka Trudy, is the daughter of Alvin and Muriel Pratt, the proprietors of Pratts Store. As the only supply outlet for miles – stocking groceries, meat, haberdashery and hardware – the store is 'a gold mine' (p.204), but Gertrude aims higher than being the daughter of a tradesman, however prosperous.

Gertrude's confidence is evident from the start. Serving the customers, she stands 'ramrod straight' (p.15), can snap string with her bare fingers – 'a telling skill' (p.14) in Sergeant Farrat's view – and provokes Elsbeth Beaumont with barely disguised smugness regarding the sorry state of the latter's fur. To Elsbeth's horror, Gertrude effectively snares her future husband by using her sexuality as bait; her mother tells him, 'You've been had – and it doesn't take too much imagination to work out how' (p.109). Gertrude also uses emotional blackmail to override William's understandable misgivings regarding the alacrity of the courtship: 'I thought you loved me. What about my reputation?' (p.117).

Gertrude is desperate to make the transition from shopkeeper's daughter to the mistress of Windswept Crest. After the wedding, she assumes a new moniker – Trudy – and her vowels take on an unaccustomed roundness. She returns from a shopping trip to Melbourne with an expensive wardrobe, as well as bold plans for both the homestead and the town itself. Like Lady Macbeth, 'the ambitious soldier's wife' (p.270), Trudy manipulates her husband in order to further her own ambitions. Her chief objective is to depose Elsbeth and rule Windswept Crest through William. Significantly, her improvements to the property – the croquet lawn, the tennis court and the new stables – do not include a new tractor for her husband.

Trudy's aspirations to improve Dungatar's social standing, as well as her own, are exposed as ridiculous when her career as a director crashes to an ignominious end. Further, her ambitions have significant ramifications for the townspeople when their preoccupation with the eisteddfod allows Tilly to capitalise on their absence and set the fire. Trudy is a disgraced figure in the end, stripped of her authority and rejected by her disillusioned husband.

Evan Pettyman

Key quotes

'He was a good councillor who got things done. He also knew how every man earned his keep.' (p.58)

'The man wasn't very successful at anything, but told everyone he was.' (Tilly, p.256).

Councillor Evan Pettyman is the shire president and 'Dungatar's richest man' (p.204). Opportunistic and self-interested, Pettyman marries the daughter of the town's previous shire president for her money. To all appearances, Pettyman is a solicitous husband, treating Marigold with respect; in reality, he infantilises his wife and ensures her compliancy by dosing her with 'tonic' (p.59). Their marriage is based on deception as Pettyman is a serial adulterer, primarily concerned with his own gratification.

Equally, Pettyman shows a callous disregard for both his hapless mistress, Molly Dunnage, and her illegitimate child, demonstrating his vindictiveness when he is instrumental in sending Tilly away after Stewart's death. Although Pettyman pays for his daughter's schooling, this is in the expectation that she repay her 'benefactor' (p.158). He seems to regard Tilly's return to Dungatar as a personal affront, showing his contempt by spitting at her on the night of the ball.

In his arrogance, Pettyman vastly underestimates his fragile wife and 'clever' daughter (p.257). Ultimately though, he is his own worst enemy. After his sudden demise, the police's startling discovery of drugs, pornography and even evidence of embezzlement exposes Pettyman's criminal activities, thus destroying what remains of his reputation in the town.

Marigold Pettyman

Key quote

> 'Marigold was a shrill, whippet-like woman with a startled bearing and a nervous rash on her neck.' (p.57)

Like Molly Dunnage before her, Marigold was 'easily swept off her feet by [the] ambitious, conniving and charm-wielding' Evan Pettyman (p.256). She had been a 'shy, innocent little thing' (p.58) when she fell pregnant with their son Stewart. Later she tells Evan, 'If it weren't for him I wouldn't have had to marry you, I may have woken up to you' (p.258).

After the death of her only child, Marigold becomes a rather pathetic character, immersed in her own misery and heavily medicated to get herself through the day. She spends her time obsessively scrubbing and disinfecting her house to 'surgery standard' (p.57), keeping it in such a state of pristine cleanliness that the presence of guests instigates a panic attack.

Marigold appears to be the only person in Dungatar who does not know of Tilly's paternity. Befuddled by a toxic combination of grief and drugs, she seems unable – or unwilling – to accept the truth, consoling herself with the illusion that Evan is a devoted husband. Similarly, she idealises her dead son and deludes herself as to the manner of his death. When Tilly finally liberates her from Evan's lies, Marigold is empowered to take a deadly revenge on her treacherous husband, asserting that 'I've been under a lot of pressure for many years ... They'd understand completely' (p.258).

Elsbeth Beaumont

Key quote

> 'She was a small, sharp, razor-thin woman with a long nose and an imperious expression.' (p.16)

Elsbeth is a proud, condescending woman who jealously guards her status as the head of Dungatar's leading family. A farmer's daughter who married a grazier's son, she was disappointed to discover that he wasn't as affluent as she had imagined. This has led to an ongoing cash-flow problem as the Beaumonts live well beyond their means. Subsequently, Elsbeth has invested all of her hopes in her son William, whom she hopes will restore the fortunes of Windswept Crest. When he marries a woman his mother considers far beneath him, Elsbeth derives no satisfaction in being reinstated to 'her rightful place' (p.109) in the family hierarchy.

Nevertheless, Elsbeth and her new daughter-in-law do have ambition in common, and the pair briefly form a tenuous alliance. They are united in their grand plans for Dungatar and their readiness to use the newly formed Social Club as a mechanism to improve the Beaumont family's coffers. Predictably, Elsbeth never gets over her dislike of the 'grocer's girl' (p.213). Their mutual rivalry resurfaces in rehearsals for *Macbeth* during which, unable to pull rank, Elsbeth washes her hands of the whole production. Her contempt for the 'loathsome' cast – 'I hope I never set eyes on any of you ever again' (p.273) – backfires, however, when she is forced to offer the townspeople hospitality after Dungatar is destroyed by fire.

Beula Harridene

Key quote

> 'You sure got shit on your liver today Mrs, you musta sunk a power of piss last night.' (George McSwiney, p.50)

Beula is malice personified; an angry, spiteful individual who carries an obsessive grudge against humanity in general, and Tilly Dunnage in particular. Her only friend appears to be Lois Pickett, with whom she runs the Saturday-morning cake stall – an initiative that presents Beula with ample opportunity to scrutinise and criticise her neighbours from the sidelines. Beula's regular visits to Sergeant Farrat with her list of grievances – 'full of hate and accusations' (p.95) – becomes an unwelcome feature of his day.

Beula is the only woman in Dungatar who resists the lure of Tilly's talents, refusing to demean herself by having a dress made by the woman she calls 'the murderess' (p.46). Her hatred of Tilly is pathological and has no apparent boundaries. At the ball, Beula even takes unscrupulous pleasure in telling Marigold the name of Tilly's father – because Marigold has been crowned 'Belle of the Ball' in a gown '*she*' made (p.182).

The final image of Beula is of a wretched figure who has, literally, lost her bearings. Packed off to a sanatorium in Melbourne, Beula has a tag pinned on the back of her cardigan in case she gets lost and a white cane to help her navigate her shadowy way. For a woman who has deliberately rejected the light of goodness in people, instead seeing evil and darkness at every turn, her fate seems apposite.

THEMES, IDEAS & VALUES

Community

Key quotes

'You can't keep anything secret here ...' (Molly, p.33)

'In this town a man can covet his neighbour's wife and not get hurt, but to speak the truth can earn a bleeding nose.' (Septimus, p.141)

In *The Dressmaker*, Ham shows us the two mutually exclusive faces of the Dungatar community. Farrat reminds the congregation at Teddy's funeral of the importance of tolerance, and it could be argued that Dungatar – with the obvious exception of attitudes to the Dunnages – is surprisingly inclusive and accepting of difference. The town has its fair share of oddities, such as Septimus Crescant – who was dropped on his head as a baby and promotes 'his Flat Earth Society' (p.67) – and the train-obsessed Hamish O'Brien, as well as the unconventional domestic arrangements of various residents. Equally, although the McSwineys are described as 'outcasts' by virtue of their impoverished social position, they are still respected as worthy and hard-working; Teddy is lionised once he proves himself an 'asset' (p.197).

Moreover, it would be simplistic to suggest that the town does not welcome outsiders per se. Many – such as Evan Pettyman and Muriel Pratt – are not originally from Dungatar, but have become valued members of the local community. Muriel tells her daughter that she moved to Dungatar expressly to escape the snobbery of South Yarra (p.150). Farrat's appeal to the townspeople's magnanimity reflects his own personal experience. Despite the narrowness of small-town life, Dungatar has provided a refuge for the eccentric policeman who, ironically, is allowed to fly under the radar, far from the scrutiny of the Melbourne police force. Sexual deviance, like moral questionability or social aberrance, is good-naturedly absorbed into the fabric of the town.

This disparate community is drawn together by football. Its importance to Dungatar's residents is established in the opening chapter when Sergeant Farrat correctly gauges the subdued mood of the town, in anticipation of a critical match the following day. With the possible exception of Beula Harridene, the whole community is invested in Dungatar's success on the field. When the team wins the cup – for the first time since before the war – the town is ecstatic. Converging on the Station Hotel, the locals celebrate until dawn, singing and dancing 'in various stages of undress and inebriation' (p.67).

The impromptu game of kick-to-kick started by Teddy on the fundraising day at Windswept Crest sees the Dungatar community at its best: loyal, good-humoured and intolerant of humbug, having sabotaged the Beaumonts' pretentions by converting the croquet lawn into a footy field. While Elsbeth dismisses the townspeople's enjoyment – 'It's always the way with the rabble' (p.152) – the camaraderie that spawns the game is undeniable.

The other side of Dungatar – the side that is shown to the Dunnages – is vicious, close-minded and unforgiving. Beneath superficial bonhomie, this insular community feeds on gossip – the more prurient the better. Bigotry and malice flourish. Unsavoury activities occur behind closed doors, and appearances cannot be trusted. If football represents unity and tribalism, it also becomes a metaphor for conflict, with winners, losers and sacrifices. The 'close and dirty battle' (p.65) with rivals Winyerp foreshadows the larger struggle between Tilly and Dungatar, with Teddy – elevated to heroic status after scoring the winning point in the final – caught in the middle. After casting himself as Tilly's champion, Teddy is positioned as a potential antagonist of the town, but his death enables Dungatar to reclaim him as 'our hero' (p.194).

With Dungatar's treatment of the Dunnages, Ham turns the stereotypical image of the warm-hearted country community on its head. Mother and daughter are easy targets. They are vulnerable to criticism as single women living outside the conventional social boundaries, and subsequent tragedy only hardens the town's animosity towards them. Tilly tells the sergeant: 'The people ... never will forgive me for that boy's death or my mother's mistakes' (pp.191–2). The text highlights the ugly power of the mob, with the majority succumbing to a pack mentality in rejecting the pair. The fact that Mae McSwiney and Irma Almanac hid their support of Molly during the years of Tilly's absence indicates their reluctance to defy the prevailing mood. After Teddy's death, Dungatar closes ranks in its collective persecution of the Dunnages.

The community's inherent dysfunctionality is showcased by its unsuccessful attempt to mount a production of *Macbeth*. A ghastly comedy of errors rather than a bonding exercise, the production is fraught with arguments and misunderstandings, petty grievances and jealousies, underlining the townspeople's inability to work together. The ultimate performance is so woeful they are not allowed to continue beyond Act I. While the account of this doomed enterprise has a farcical side, the novel is serious in its contention that the greatest threat to a community can come from within. Abandoning respect and goodwill in favour of vindictiveness and blame has irreparably damaged the social contract, and the residents of Dungatar pay a heavier price for this than just their humiliation at the drama competition.

Key point

The two hills – the privileged Beaumonts' Windswept Crest (Fart Hill) and The Hill, where the Dunnages live – represent the polarised faces of Dungatar. The first embodies social acceptance; the second, social exclusion.

Gender roles

Key quotes

'... these are progressive times – it's an advantage to be adept, especially in the fairer sex ...' (Farrat, p.14)

He paused a moment to run his hands over his nylon stockings and admire his new lace panties.' (p.45)

Australia in the 1950s is a patriarchal culture, with male privilege and women's vulnerability very much on show. Women and men – in particular wealthy, powerful men – are judged differently. Men can, and often do, exploit their power over women.

Different standards also apply to sexual behaviour. Women are expected to be virgins before they marry, but almost the opposite applies to men. Both Gertrude Pratt and Mona Beaumont find themselves in situations that are potentially compromising. When it appears that Mona and Lesley have been intimate, Elsbeth's response is unequivocal: 'You'll have to marry her' (p.159). Trudy is more calculating than Mona and understands the transactional nature of male/female relationships. She gambles on William's sense of propriety and, when he suggests postponing the wedding, successfully blackmails him into honouring his end of the bargain.

Marriage confers respectability, but also a sense of ownership. Fred Bundle has helped his wife – 'all bright and blonde and barmaidy' (p.128) – to bury her promiscuous past but, as her saviour, keeps a territorial watch on 'his Purly' (p.27). Fred is prepared to be magnanimous about previous relationships, including Purl's liaison with Bill Beaumont, as long as Purl – and everyone else – understands his present claim: 'MY Purl' (p.64).

Evan Pettyman's shameful treatment of his wife exemplifies the prevailing double standard in relation to gender. As well as stealing Marigold's money, Pettyman is an inveterate womaniser, even sleeping with Una Pleasance when she is staying with the Pettymans. He is a predator who gropes his unwilling dance partners, 'ramming his thigh between their legs to move them around the floor' (p.57). The local women avoid him where possible, while the men tolerate his behaviour, making excuses for him because of his power as shire president. Tilly's paternity is an open secret in Dungatar but, although Molly is shamed for having a child outside marriage, the councillor continues to command respect.

Pettyman's treatment of Molly effectively ruins her life. She is an inexperienced young woman when he seduces her, and he pursues her ruthlessly when she tries to extricate herself from the relationship. After Stewart's death, he uses his considerable influence to punish her in the cruellest way possible by having her child sent away and not divulging

Tilly's whereabouts. Molly's situation highlights the way that women's financial dependency robs them of choice. With 'no money, no job and an illegitimate child to support' (p.232), she is powerless to resist Pettyman's demands.

As well as making the decisions and controlling the purse strings, some of the men in Dungatar abuse their wives with impunity. Mr Almanac is a sadistic, judgemental bully whose wife, Irma, 'used to have a lot of falls, which left her with a black eye or a cut lip' (p.41). Moreover, he denies her the medication that would make her arthritic pain more bearable. Like Irma, Marigold Pettyman suffers abuse and indignity at the hands of her husband. Marigold is drugged and regularly subjected to marital rape. Almanac is complicit in this degradation as he provides the 'tonic' with which Pettyman controls his wife: 'Mr Almanac said you could have as much as you needed' (p.229).

Teddy represents the other side of the patriarchal coin. Motivated by love and chivalry, his instincts are to 'look after' Tilly (p.91) while still allowing her space to be herself. Teddy does not endorse the conservative values that deny women equality; he respects Tilly's talent and does not care about her past. Yet, Teddy's self-belief is such that he underestimates community sentiment. As an attractive, charming man, he is used to getting his own way, and exerts benign pressure on Tilly to go out with him, pushing her into social situations – such as the ball – that backfire, exposing her further to the townspeople's cruelty. His own death becomes another weapon to use against her.

The Dressmaker challenges the gender stereotyping of the time through the characters of Tilly and Sergeant Farrat, both of whom defy traditional expectations. Tilly is unmarried, but chose to live with a man in Europe and bear a child. While there are obvious parallels with Molly's story, Tilly has agency where her mother did not; her dressmaking skills enable her to run her own business and be financially independent. Sergeant Farrat's cross-dressing subverts the orthodox male/female paradigm. That Dungatar, with its conventional morality and propensity to judge, has been a haven for Farrat for so many years is one of the paradoxes of the novel. Not only has the policeman managed to elude criticism for his peculiarities, but in fact the townspeople are pleased that, 'unlike their former sergeant', Farrat 'didn't join the football club or insist on free beer' (p.20). Even so, depictions of the sergeant modelling his new corset or luxuriating in his bath wearing a face mask present a startling contrast to the bloodstained heroics on the football field or other archetypal images of Australian masculinity – such as the shearer and the drover – depicted in the text.

Change

Key quotes

'She wondered about what she had left behind her, and what she had returned to.' (p.9)

'Nothing ever really changes, Myrtle.' (Mae, p.77)

Dungatar seems to exist in a contextual vacuum. There is no reference to news or current events from the wider world, including the recent trauma of World War II. As a community, Dungatar looks inward. The interests of the townspeople extend only as far as the neighbouring towns of Winyerp and Itheca. Hamish O'Brien exemplifies the general resistance to change when he laments the fact that his beloved steam engines are being replaced by diesel (p.70).

Tilly's arrival into this parochial bubble presents a challenge in addition to that posed by her personal history with the town. She represents a fresh perspective and a more sophisticated world view, having travelled widely in Europe at a time of social upheaval. From Dungatar's perspective, everything about Tilly is different: what she wears, eats and reads, and the music she listens to.

Back in her home town, Tilly's world contracts. She recognises Dungatar's suspicion of anything new or unfamiliar, correcting Teddy's well-meaning but simplistic assertion that the town will need to change in order to accommodate her: 'No … I'll have to get used to them' (p.91). Yet Tilly is an agent for change, the catalyst that will shake Dungatar out of its complacency. Survival has been the driving imperative in her life of adaptation and reinvention – change has mainly been forced on her by adverse circumstances – but she has also been motivated by inspirational mentors and a hunger for success.

Tilly's dressmaking ability is her means to connect with the town. Throughout *The Dressmaker*, Ham explores the language and symbolic significance of clothes. When Tilly first returns to Dungatar, everyone takes note of what she is wearing – her glamorous, modish wardrobe is the single most obvious sign of the extent to which she herself has changed. She is able to build on this curiosity by offering the town a talent that is desirable and rare.

Fashion, by definition, is based on the idea of change. Feeding an appetite for the new and the different, it is a platform for women to use their imagination and explore their fantasies. Though Tilly's work reflects the influence of her haute couture teachers, she is an original creator who often eschews the traditional clichés – the 'ruffs and flounces' (p.148) – of femininity. Instead, her designs celebrate the individual female form. When Trudy and Elsbeth return from Melbourne, their copied Dior skirts, 'huge and domed in yards and yards of taffeta' (p.135), present a marked contrast to Muriel's simple but very chic linen tunic, designed by Tilly. Tilly works a kind of alchemy on the women of Dungatar who are 'renovated, European-touched, advanced to almost avante-garde [*sic*]' (p.153) by her skill and imagination. The visitor from Melbourne is confounded, wondering 'how Paris had found its way to the dilapidated confines and neglected torsos of banal housewives in a rural province' (p.165).

At its best, fashion is depicted as an exciting form of self-expression, an opportunity to showcase personal style and creativity. The novel acknowledges fashion's power to transform while, at the same time, underscoring its limitations. Like the work of all great couturiers, Tilly's designs present each individual in the most flattering guise. Unfortunately, the women of Dungatar are motivated by vanity and one-upmanship. While they flaunt Tilly's elegant designs, their understanding of style is one-dimensional and the clothes can only effect a superficial transformation, beneath which Dungatar continues to be 'a town of round shoulders and splayed gaits' (p.171). Worse, these women remain as small-minded and ungenerous as ever, continuing to treat Tilly selfishly and cruelly even as they exploit her expertise. Teddy maintains that the new wardrobes have had a regrettable effect on her clients who have 'grown airs, think they're classy' (p.175).

Moreover, the townspeople's inability to change is directly related to their readiness to deceive themselves. Gertrude Pratt is a prime example. Her radiant transformation on her wedding day owes everything to Tilly's wizardry in disguising the bride's lumpy thighs and square bottom while showcasing her slender waist. However, Gertrude's new persona brings arrogance and a false sense of entitlement; predictably, she becomes a victim of her own narcissism. Morphing into 'Trudy', she decides that, under her direction, her home town can do better: 'We're going to take *Doongatah* for the ride of its life' (p.136). Trudy's all-consuming self-belief allows her to disregard inconvenient facts and, by sheer force of personality, she carries others along with her. The idea that a successful production of *Macbeth* can be mounted with an inexperienced cast – some of whom have never heard of Shakespeare – is exposed as a pretentious delusion. The elaborate baroque costumes cannot transform them into capable actors; they are simply revealed as vain and foolish.

Similarly, the townspeople's predilection to pervert the truth when it suits them and their refusal to listen to reason are fundamental obstacles to meaningful growth. At Teddy's funeral, Sergeant Farrat points out that, like Tilly, Teddy was also an outcast, 'until he proved himself an asset' (p.197). In vain, Farrat argues that Teddy wanted the townspeople to love Tilly and considered the way she had been treated 'unforgivable' (p.197). Dungatar remains fixed in its view that Tilly is a murderer. Cocooned in their insularity, the townspeople reject the need to rethink attitudes and behaviours that have spanned a generation.

In the end, after changing the landscape of the town in the most conclusive way, it is Tilly who again moves on to start a new life. Her going-away outfit is significant. The blouse, 'delicate and simple' (p.289), is sewn from nun's veiling (p.290), highlighting the way in which something pedestrian can be transformed into something unexpectedly beautiful. It exemplifies not only Tilly's artistry, but also her talent for adaptation, and is the antithesis of the cumbersome, impractical baroque regalia, which is all the townspeople have left to call their own.

Key point

The novel demonstrates that change is only of value – or even possible – when there is a genuine understanding of self and a willingness to address uncomfortable truths. This applies at both a personal and a societal level.

Victimisation

Key quotes

'"Something's burning my back," said Molly. "You should be used to it by now," said Tilly.' (p.39)

'Everyone likes to have someone to hate.' (Tilly, p.175)

In *The Dressmaker*, Dungatar's tendency to attribute blame and victimise the innocent is strong. Convention and respectability form the basis of Dungatar's creed, and Molly Dunnage committed the cardinal sin of having a child out of wedlock. In the town's eyes, this is her real crime, not her relationship with Evan Pettyman. At the same time, victimisation of the Dunnages is selective. Ham is highly critical of the hypocrisy that allows the town to turn a blind eye to other immoral behaviour, such as Faith O'Brien's adultery with Reginald Blood. By contrast, Molly is judged and condemned for her sexual history, and has been ostracised as 'mad' (p.232) and immoral ever since Tilly's birth.

Dungatar's judgement extends to Tilly, the tangible evidence of Molly's transgression. The vulnerable child is treated shamefully by the townspeople. She is bullied and reviled at school. The teacher, Prudence Dimm, sets the tone by spitefully persecuting Tilly, physically abusing her and repeatedly singling her out for ink-well duty. Miss Dimm's example encourages her suggestible students to be equally cruel. In the playground, Tilly is called 'Dunnybum' and 'a bar-std' (p.56), and children hold her arms out while Stewart Pettyman runs at her 'like a charging bull' (p.56). The hostile town convinces itself that the little girl is responsible for his subsequent death. As daughter of the shunned Molly, Tilly has no voice and no advocate. Only another outsider, Edward McSwiney, steps in on her behalf, telling Sergeant Farrat that 'the poor little thing … was just trying to save herself' (p.193). Tilly is taken from her mother and sent to Melbourne. As an added insult, Tilly is forced to refer to the man responsible for this injustice as her 'benefactor' (p.158).

When Tilly returns to the town, Molly reminds her that 'it's open slather on outcasts' (p.33). Tilly is marginalised from the moment she arrives, in a communal campaign of covert bullying. Her outsider status is reinforced by the casual cruelty with which the town turns its back on her at the dance, despite her being accompanied by Teddy. She continues to be snubbed and excluded, even from events where she has earned the right to be present. At the Pratt wedding reception, Tilly stands in darkness outside the back door, waiting for an acknowledgement of her work. To the disappointment of the female guests, the name of Gertrude's dressmaker is not mentioned. Similarly, despite making the glorious gowns paraded by the women at the ball, she has no allocated place at the event: on the seating plan, her name has been repeatedly scribbled – or even torn – out (p.183).

The town's hostility escalates to contemptible proportions after Teddy's death. Showing the same irrational bigotry as in the past, the townspeople blame Tilly. Sergeant Farrat's eulogy encourages them to love and include Tilly, as Teddy would have wanted. Instead, their malevolence intensifies. The Dunnage women are vilified as 'murderers' and 'witches' (p.201) and locals throw rocks at their house (p.201). Tilly and her mother become prisoners in their own home as the town's persecution makes it impossible for them to go out during daylight. Even the apparently good-natured Faith O'Brien shoves Tilly when she ventures into town for provisions. With the single exception of Farrat, everyone remaining in Dungatar is complicit.

Key point

The townspeople of Dungatar are intolerant and sanctimonious, quick to judge and reluctant to forgive. This creates a climate in which people give themselves permission to behave with cruelty and injustice.

Loss

Key quotes

'But then there was another … everyone I've touched is hurt, or dead.' (Tilly, p.192)

'I'd lost the only friend I had, the only thing I had, but over the years I came to hope you wouldn't come back to this awful place.' (Molly, p.233)

Loss is the unhappy current that runs through *The Dressmaker*, permeating the lives of the characters in a way that is intergenerational. In particular, the text explores the crushing effect on a parent's psyche when they experience the loss of a child. In spite of their many differences, the Dunnages, the Pettymans and the McSwineys all have this trauma in common.

Mental instability is the price paid by both Molly and Marigold. These two women are both profoundly damaged by the sudden loss of their child, retreating deep inside themselves, their perception blurred by grief. Connected through their relationship with Evan Pettyman, both are victims of the councillor's monstrous selfishness. Pettyman's realisation that his own daughter has inadvertently caused the death of her half-brother does nothing to mitigate his rage at losing the boy. He is determined to punish his mistress and the child he never wanted: Molly explains, 'when he couldn't have his son anymore, I couldn't have you' (p.232). Sergeant Farrat is sympathetic, but cannot prevail against Pettyman's malice or the mood of the town. Molly has no-one to champion her cause and, troubled and increasingly dysfunctional, she is abandoned by most of her neighbours.

In the emotionally charged confrontation immediately after Stewart's death, Molly also predicts that Pettyman will send his 'poor stupid' wife mad (p.194). This comes dangerously close to the truth. Marigold takes refuge in a shadowy world of delusion, concocting an alternative reality in which her son has fallen out of a tree and landed on his head. Interestingly, this version absolves Tilly of blame. The councillor's wife gains a reputation in the town as being 'highly strung' (p.58), and her life becomes a joyless routine of obsessive housekeeping and night-time medication.

After Teddy's untimely death, Sergeant Farrat reflects on the anguish experienced by all the grieving parents of the town, for whom every familiar street and building acts as a reminder of their loved ones. In this setting, they are denied the luxury of anonymity, and the neighbours' pity only compounds their pain: 'everywhere they looked, they could see that everyone saw them, knowing' (p.194). The McSwineys are so broken by their loss that they cannot stay in Dungatar. Before their departure, Edward destroys their once 'happy family home', which is rendered 'a crumpled shrouded black heap' (p.199).

Loss has been the defining constant in Tilly's life. Her adult life mirrors her mother's story, to some extent, with a similar pattern of deprivation and grief. Tilly establishes a successful life for herself in Paris, but it is destroyed by the unexpected death of her baby son. Compounding her misery is the response of the boy's father, who is unable to come to terms with the tragedy. In yet another example of the victim-blaming that pervades the text, Ormond holds Tilly responsible and punishes her further by deserting her.

The tangible losses that Tilly has suffered are accompanied by a more subtle but no less destructive kind of loss – that of her peace of mind. The deaths of Stewart and her son have left a permanent legacy of guilt and shame; like many victims of abuse, she blames herself. When Tilly first returns to Dungatar, Sergeant Farrat perceptively observes that she seems 'strong, but damaged' (p.7). In Dungatar, Tilly's past remains an open wound that is impossible to cauterise; the town's resentment of her is palpable and she is reminded of it whenever she drops her guard. As she explains to Teddy, her guilt is 'like a black thing – a weight ... it makes itself invisible then creeps back when I feel safest ...' (p.184).

With Teddy's death, Tilly loses the promise of a brighter future and her capacity to forgive herself is diminished even further. Initially, she is reluctant to begin a relationship because she no longer trusts herself, fearing that she is 'cursed'. While Teddy is the first to absolve her, ironically, it is his foolhardy attempt to disprove her fears that kills him. Afterwards comes despair. She feels 'she must stay in Dungatar for a kind of penance' (p.195) and considers herself 'bankrupted in all ways' (p.196), underserving of forgiveness or love.

Too late, Tilly and her mother share a brief, cathartic moment of reconciliation and love. The unexpected lucidity that follows Molly's dream of her grandson allows Tilly to tell her story and, in turn, hear her mother's. She realises the full extent of Molly's own bereavement, and the fact that powerful forces were pitted against them both. After Molly's death, Tilly again confronts a truth that has been unchanged since she was ten years old: 'I will miss you … I will just go on missing you as I always have' (p.242).

Retribution

Key quotes

'In light of all they had done, and what they had not done, what they had decided not to do – they mustn't be abandoned. Not yet.' (p.236)

'… she looks like she's been hit by the corner of a flying fridge.' (Farrat, p.246)

The Dressmaker endorses a concept of justice that is uncompromisingly Old Testament; the 'eye for an eye' principle that propels events in the text to their violent conclusion is decisive and unforgiving. In this karmic chain of events, fate sometimes lends a hand, as is the case for Beula Harridene and Mr Almanac. Ironically, both of these individuals believe vehemently in the idea of retribution, although they confuse justice with vengeance, rationalising their own cruelty. Not only does Almanac abuse his wife, he has no hesitation in inflicting pain on those he considers deserving of punishment. As the only chemist in town, he is in a position of singular power, but he perversely believes that sin is 'the cause of all disease' (p.40). His 'remedy' for Faith O'Brien's vaginal itch is the abrasive cleaning agent White Lily (p.23). Ultimately though, Parkinson's disease robs Almanac of his mobility to such a degree that he cannot even safely navigate his way home.

Similarly, Beula meets an ugly, but fitting, end. Her unrelenting malevolence tests even the tolerant Sergeant Farrat; after her attempt to incriminate the little McSwineys (pp.46–7), the policeman warns her in no uncertain terms not to waste his time. Beula's obsessive vendetta against Tilly comes to an abrupt conclusion when she is accidentally hit by the flying radiogram: 'The lights had gone out for Beula' (p.246). Her damaged, 'rotting face' (p.245) is a graphic representation of the venom that has poisoned her psyche for so long.

Collectively, Dungatar encounters its nemesis in Tilly, whose unapologetic actions result in the town's destruction. After her mother's death, Tilly's perspective shifts and, rather than accepting blame, she starts to apportion it. On Molly's behalf as much as her own, Tilly vows retribution against the town: 'Pain will no longer be our curse ... It will be our revenge and our reason' (p.236). Tilly's campaign commences with Evan Pettyman, proving that truth is a powerful weapon when it can be heard. In a neat act of poetic justice, Tilly's herbal concoction effectively emasculates Pettyman so that Marigold is able to take her own vengeance on her faithless husband. Watching with satisfaction as Evan bleeds to death on her polished floor, Marigold phlegmatically states that people would 'understand completely' (p.258).

Tilly's incineration of the whole town is carefully calculated. She sets the fire on a hot, windy day when the fire brigade is absent, making sure that her own house will burn quickly by stuffing it to the rafters with inflammable material and dousing it with kerosene. As a final touch, she turns off the water. By the time the actors return from the disastrous eisteddfod, Dungatar is 'black and smoking' (p.294). Reduced to 'terrified children lost in a crowd' (p.295), the townspeople can only survey the damage while digesting the unpalatable fact that their insurance premiums have not been paid.

On face value, Tilly's destruction of Dungatar is an immoral choice. Yet we are positioned to empathise with the protagonist and see her intervention as just. She is presented as a righteous figure, surrounded by light. As she prepares to set the fire that will cleanse Dungatar of its vitriol, she is 'wreathed in a brilliant halo, like a back-lit actor, dust from tailor's chalk and flock floating in shafts of light about her' (p.286). Furthermore, Tilly evades any consequences that may result from her actions; by escaping to Melbourne, she is essentially exonerated.

The battle lines are clearly delineated in *The Dressmaker*. Tilly's reprisal is extreme, allowing no room for prevarication or mercy. The arson is indiscriminate and includes destroying the homes of her few friends – gentle Irma Almanac and the loyal Sergeant Farrat – as well as her many enemies. However, Ham elicits little sympathy for the citizens of Dungatar. Malice and blind prejudice have been their undoing and, in this sense, they have brought the crisis on themselves. Perhaps in the future, the town will make the choice to rebuild itself as a community where love and compassion, rather than hate, prevail.

DIFFERENT INTERPRETATIONS

Different interpretations arise from different responses to a text. Over time, a text will evoke a wide range of responses from its readers, who may come from various social or cultural groups and live in very different places and historical periods. Responses by critics and reviewers can be published in newspapers, journals and books, both online and in print. They can also be expressed in discussions among readers in the media, classrooms, book groups and so on.

While there is no single correct reading or interpretation of a text, it is important to understand that an interpretation is more than a personal opinion – it is the justification of a point of view on a text. To present an interpretation of a text based on your point of view, you must use a logical argument and support it with relevant evidence from the text.

Critical viewpoints

The critical reception that *The Dressmaker* received when it was first published was very favourable. Reviewers were united in their praise of Ham's finely honed eye for the absurd and the way in which she captures the parochial bigotry of rural Australia in the 1950s. In her review for *Compulsive Reader*, Ruth Latta calls the novel 'a clever satire about village life' (Latta 2015), while Daneet Steffens in *The Boston Globe* writes that 'the book's true pleasures involve the way Rosalie Ham has small-town living down pat' (Steffens 2015).

Writing for *The New York Times*, Kate Clanchy compliments 'Ham's arch, polished prose' and maintains that she has real gifts as a descriptive writer, 'bringing Tilly's frocks to surprising, animated life' (Clanchy 2015). Diana Simmonds in *The Weekend Australian* agrees, praising Ham's 'delightfully rich set pieces and descriptive passages' (Simmonds 2000).

However, some reviewers have also identified an unevenness of tone. Clanchy notes a tension between the 'taffeta-thin, tulle-bright world' that Ham so successfully creates and the gritty reality of Tilly's oppressive past, and calls the revenge ending 'problematic'. Equally, Joanne Wilkes, in the *New Zealand Herald*, contends that 'the novel's changes in tone from black comedy to pathos are not always well-handled' (Wilkes 2001). On the other hand, Steffens praises the way the novel 'exposes both the dark and the shimmering lights in our human hearts', calling it 'a compelling mix of magical and surreal elements'.

Two interpretations of *The Dressmaker*

Interpretation 1: *The Dressmaker* is essentially a black comedy that invites us to laugh at the foibles of human nature.

The tone of *The Dressmaker* is essentially satirical. Its broad range of characters runs the gamut from endearing to appalling, and Ham exposes their flaws with derisive mockery. In spite of its moments of tragedy, the novel never loses its darkly comic edge.

In the main, it is the foolishness of the characters that is emphasised, rather than their villainy. Much of the comedy arises out of the juxtaposition of Tilly's sophistication and the townspeople's ignorance. When Tilly's large tea-chest arrives from Europe, Ruth Dimm takes it upon herself to go through its contents. The foreign recipes, photos, postcards and books represent a world that is a complete mystery to the postmistress; after reading a couple of pages by 'someone called Hemingway', she finds 'no romance so tossed it aside' (p.71). Ruth and her friend Nancy Pickett sleep 'like babies' after consuming Tilly's 'green, weedy stuff' (presumably cannabis, p.75), but have less success with the substance they are subsequently told is 'South American Vampire bat dung' – in reality, henna (p.76).

The Dressmaker certainly includes episodes of great sadness and poignancy. The confronting Part III, Felt, which deals with the deaths of Teddy and Molly, falls into this category. However, the novel always returns to the black humour that is at its core, and Part IV, Brocade, reclaims its satirical tone. Ham's response to the genuinely miserable moments is to offset them with events that are often so grotesque as to be almost risible (absurd).

After the wretchedness of Molly's death and her lonely funeral, Tilly and Sergeant Farrat carouse together and get very drunk in Molly's memory. As viewed through Beula's jaundiced perspective, the spontaneous wake features too much alcohol, a mutilated Bible and the sergeant in a dress. The revelry culminates in Tilly throwing the radiogram out the window, whereupon it hits the hapless Beula in the face. However, despite the seriousness of Beula's injuries, the element of farce balances out any horror we may feel. This is the first of a spate of accidents towards the end of the text that are presented with similar gallows humour. The truly malevolent characters – Beula Harridene, Mr Almanac and Evan Pettyman – receive their comeuppance in such macabre ways that it is difficult to view these events as anything other than grimly satisfying. When Sergeant Farrat fishes Mr Almanac out of his watery grave, the latter has 'slimy green cumbungi streaming from his bent neck, yabbies clinging to his ear lobes and leeches hanging from his lips' (p.248). Evan Pettyman's death is described in equally gleeful terms. As Marigold calmly slashes his ankles, Evan goes down 'trumpeting like a tortured elephant' while his Achilles tendons shrink 'to coil like snuggled slugs in the capsular ligaments behind his knee joints' (p.258).

Nowhere is the folly of the townspeople more on show than in the Dungatar Social Club's decision to mount a production of *Macbeth*. While Tilly can quote verbatim from the play, the cultural illiteracy of the committee members becomes immediately apparent. Mona is probably not the only one who had never heard of Shakespeare until the previous week. Hamish O'Brien, who is in charge of props, seems to be confused as to which play they are staging (p.269). And Bobby Pickett, keen to understand the text, wants to know where 'damned' Spot (p.273) – presumably a dog – might be.

The citizens of Dungatar may be heading for a well-deserved fall, but in the meantime, we are positioned to laugh at their ill-fated endeavours. This section of the novel, in fact, has more in common with one of

Shakespeare's own comedies – indirectly referencing *A Midsummer Night's Dream* and the mechanicals' attempt to stage their riotously off-the-mark production of 'Pyramus and Thisbe'.

Similarly, the ending of *The Dressmaker* is more farce than tragedy. Having 'been burned out of existence' (p.295), the response of the townspeople is typically mercurial. First, they bawl like children, then Scotty Pullit decides they might as well have a drink and finally, with misplaced optimism, they adopt Mona's sly suggestion to inflict themselves on Elsbeth Beaumont. Absurdly, despite losing everything, we are reminded that the cast still have their 'very effective Baroque costumes' (p.296). The final image of this 'motley bunch' (p.296) lumbering hopefully up Fart Hill is comical in its incongruity.

Interpretation 2: *The Dressmaker* is a darkly pessimistic novel, with an overwhelmingly bleak view of human nature.

The Dressmaker presents a cynical picture of life in a small country town and the people who reside there. Comic relief is provided in some instances where Ham ridicules the foibles of the townspeople, but overwhelmingly the tone of the novel is pessimistic. There are few uplifting moments or truly likable characters. Even those individuals who evoke some sympathy are flawed. Molly Dunnage – herself a difficult, embittered woman – dismisses everyone in Dungatar as 'liars, sinners and hypocrites' (p.175).

This pessimistic tone is established from the outset. Tilly's homecoming is far from happy – her own mother views her as an unwanted stranger and the townspeople react with contempt. Dungatar is an intolerant, spiteful community where hypocrisy and self-interest prevail. Faith O'Brien and her 'goings on' (p.100) are common knowledge in the town, as is Nancy Pickett's relationship with the postmistress, yet these same women join the rest of the town in denouncing Molly as a slut.

The town's demonisation of the Dunnage women exposes a bleak aspect of human nature; the ill-treatment of Tilly and her mother is the result of an entrenched, collective prejudice that leads to blame and injustice. The extent of Dungatar's 'anger and woe' (p.205) after Teddy's death makes Tilly fear for her safety. Listening to supporters watching the football without their beloved full forward, she imagines them streaming up The Hill with 'clenched fists for revenge blood' (p.205).

Many of the characters are presented as irredeemably awful. Looking at her mannequins, Tilly is reminded of 'snobby old Elsbeth and canvas water-bag Gertrude, and puny Mona or putrid gossiping Lois, leathery old sticky-beak Ruth, venomous Beula' (p.200). In spite of their contemptible behaviour towards her and their transparent lack of remorse, when these erstwhile clients need a good dressmaker again, they simply expect to pick up Tilly's services as if nothing had happened.

In Dungatar, there is little trust and even less loyalty. Alliances are formed out of expediency, rather than affection or altruism. The chaotic scene in which Trudy unexpectedly goes into labour highlights the fragility of the Beaumont family relationships. As Trudy delivers her baby on the Pettymans' living-room floor, she and Elsbeth scream invective at each other – 'SHUT UP, you stupid grocer's girl' / 'This is all your son's fault, you old witch' (pp.213–14) – showing the true aversion they feel for each other. Too late, William recognises that he has been manipulated into marriage by the conniving Gertrude: 'I don't really love my wife' (p.220).

Even the 'good' characters are ultimately shown to be compromised by their own weaknesses. Neither of Tilly's allies – Sergeant Farrat and Teddy McSwiney – are able to offer her the support she needs. Though sympathetic, Farrat seems to accept the prevailing wisdom of separating Tilly from her mother after Stewart's death: 'We will have to take Myrtle away' (p.194). He is equally ineffective after Teddy's death, unable to dissuade the people from their 'continuing hatred' (p.201). Teddy's recklessness, in fact, compounds Tilly's woes. By throwing away his life and their future together in a childish demonstration of showmanship, he damages her reputation further in the eyes of the townspeople.

Tilly is a deeply troubled heroine whose life has been one of unrelenting misery. She suffers a traumatic childhood and, as an adult, her every chance of happiness seems to be snatched away. After the loss of Teddy she is 'exhausted, but her mind [races] with venom and hate for herself and the people of Dungatar' (pp.198–9). It is not surprising that she too becomes infected by their example, deciding that the town will pay for its sins of vindictiveness and cruelty.

Tilly exploits the townspeople's weaknesses, using their pride and ignorance against them. She plants the seed of the play, knowing that the Social Club cannot resist showing up its neighbours, and she encourages Trudy's choice of the ridiculous – and expensive – costumes. When Tilly sets the fire, it is in the knowledge that the residents have, foolishly, chosen to pay for stage costumes instead of their insurance. Dungatar's citizens may well be undone by their own culpability and refusal to forgive. Arguably though, in destroying her home town in its entirety, Tilly behaves in a way that is just as unforgiving and vengeful.

The ending to *The Dressmaker* is essentially bleak – there are many losers, but no real winners. Virtue is not rewarded in this text. Tilly may escape from Dungatar, but she leaves in the same way she arrived, alone and friendless; her sole companion is the caged galah (p.290). The only people who truly loved her are dead, and her future is uncertain. All she retains is the sense of isolation that has dogged her most of her life.

QUESTIONS & ANSWERS

This section focuses on your own analytical writing on the text, and gives you strategies for producing high-quality responses in your coursework and exam essays.

Essay writing – an overview

An essay on a literary work is a formal and serious piece of writing that presents your point of view on the text, usually in response to a given topic. Your 'point of view' in an essay is your interpretation of the meaning of the text's language, structure, characters, situations and events, supported by detailed analysis of textual evidence.

Analyse – don't summarise

In your essays it is important to avoid simply summarising what happens in a text.

- A **summary** is a description or paraphrase (retelling in different words) of the characters and events. For example: 'Macbeth has a horrifying vision of a dagger dripping with blood before he goes to murder King Duncan.'
- An **analysis** is an explanation of the real meaning or significance that lies 'beneath' the text's words (and images, for a film). For example: 'Macbeth's vision of a bloody dagger shows how deeply uneasy he is about the violent act he is contemplating, and conveys his sense that supernatural forces are impelling him to act.'

A limited amount of summary is sometimes necessary to let your reader know which part of the text you wish to discuss. However, always keep this to a minimum and follow it immediately with your analysis of what this part of the text is really telling us.

Plan your essay

Carefully plan your essay so that you have a clear idea of what you are going to say. The plan ensures that your ideas flow logically, that your argument remains consistent and that you stay on the topic. An essay plan should be a list of **brief dot points** covering no more than half a page.

- Include your central argument or main contention – a concise statement of your overall response to the topic.
- Write three or four dot points for each paragraph, indicating the main idea and evidence/examples from the text. Note that in your essay you will need to *expand* on these points and *analyse* the evidence.

Structure your essay

An essay is a complete, self-contained piece of writing. It has a clear beginning (the introduction), middle (several body paragraphs) and end (the last paragraph or conclusion). It must also have a central argument that runs throughout, linking each paragraph to form a coherent whole. See examples of introductions and conclusions in the 'Analysing a sample topic' and 'Sample answer' sections.

The introduction establishes your overall response to the topic. It includes your main contention and outlines the main evidence you will refer to in the course of the essay. Write your introduction *after* you have done a plan and *before* you write the rest of the essay.

The body paragraphs argue your case – they present evidence from the text and explain how this evidence supports your argument. Each body paragraph needs:

- a strong **topic sentence** (usually the first sentence) that states the main point being made in the paragraph
- **evidence** from the text, including some brief quotations
- **analysis** of the textual evidence, with **explanation** of its significance and how it supports your argument
- **links back to the topic** in one or more statements, usually towards the end of the paragraph.

Connect the body paragraphs so that your discussion flows smoothly. Use some linking words and phrases such as 'similarly' and 'on the other hand', though don't start every paragraph like this. Another strategy is to use a significant word from the last sentence of one paragraph in the first sentence of the next.

Use key terms from the topic – or synonyms for them – throughout, so the relevance of your discussion to the topic is always clear.

The conclusion ties everything together and finishes the essay. It includes strong statements that emphasise your central argument and provide a clear response to the topic.

Avoid simply restating the points made earlier in the essay – this will end on a very flat note and imply that you have run out of ideas and vocabulary. The conclusion should be a logical extension of what you have written, not just a repetition or summary of it. Writing an effective conclusion can be a challenge. Try using these tips:

- Start by linking back to the final sentence of the second-last paragraph rather than leaping back to your main contention straight away – this helps your writing to flow.
- Use synonyms and expressions with equivalent meanings to vary your vocabulary. This allows you to reinforce your line of argument without being repetitive.
- When planning your essay, think of one or two broad statements or observations about the text's wider meaning. These should be related to the topic and your overall argument. Keep them for the conclusion, since they will give you something 'new' to say but still follow logically from your discussion. The introduction will be focused on the topic, but the conclusion can present a wider view of the text.

Essay topics

1. 'In *The Dressmaker*, the women are stronger than the men.' Do you agree?
2. 'The characters in this text fall into two categories; they are either heroes or villains.' Discuss.
3. How does *The Dressmaker* explore the relationship between the past and the present?
4. 'In *The Dressmaker*, everyone has their place.' Do you agree?
5. 'Tilly is a troubled heroine whose actions do not always engender sympathy.' Do you agree?
6. "Everyone likes to have someone to hate." Does *The Dressmaker* show this to be true?
7. 'The people of Dungatar are punished far more than they deserve.' Do you agree?
8. How important is the concept of forgiveness in this novel?
9. '*The Dressmaker* suggests that fate is more of a factor in the lives of the characters than self-determination.' Discuss.
10. 'In this text, everything is a trade-off.' Discuss.

Vocabulary for writing on *The Dressmaker*

Gothic: in literature, Gothic is a type of fiction that explores strange or macabre events, building an atmosphere of horror and dread.

Haute couture: literally 'high fashion'; designing and creating exclusive, custom-made clothes for an individual client; usually sewn by hand using expensive, often unusual fabrics.

Intertextuality: the deliberate referencing of other texts within a text – either directly, by allusion or quotation, or indirectly by paraphrase or imitation.

Linear structure: a narrative that presents events in chronological order.

Magic / magical realism: a genre that depicts a realistic view of the world, while also adding magical or supernatural elements to the narrative.

Motif: a recurring image used to link ideas and reinforce themes; adds cohesion and unity to the writing.

Omniscient narration: an all-seeing, all-knowing narrator who presents as much or as little as they choose regarding the characters' feelings, actions and circumstances.

Patriarchy: a society whose power structures – political, religious, legal and domestic – are all invested in men.

Romance: a narrative that explores a romantic relationship between individuals.

Satire: a style of writing that uses humour and exaggeration to highlight and criticise human foibles.

Analysing a sample topic

"Everyone likes to have someone to hate."
Does *The Dressmaker* show this to be true?

This question focuses on relationships in the novel, asking you to analyse the way in which the characters interact with each other. You are asked a direct question here – you must answer it! Make your contention clear in the introduction and indicate your line of argument.

- Identify the topic quote and consider the context in which it appears (p.175). Is Tilly being bitter, ironic or philosophical? Should we take what she says at face value? To what extent does her own experience bear out the truth of this statement?
- Is 'everyone' in Dungatar motivated by hate, dislike or disapproval for 'someone'? If so, why? What does this suggest about human nature – especially life in a small country town?
- How does such a response manifest itself? What are the consequences that flow from the choices made by various characters?

- Avoid adopting too rigid a position. It is often difficult to substantiate 'black-and-white' responses; nor do they acknowledge the complexity implicit in the question.
- Do not make your answer too Tilly-centric. Look across the text at all the characters.

The following plan is only *one* way to tackle the topic; you could certainly give more weight to the argument that *all* the characters in the text are *not* well-intentioned.

Sample introduction

> *The Dressmaker*, by Rosalie Ham, proffers a cynical view of human interaction. In the main, relationships are based on self-interest and expediency, rather than tolerance or compassion. In this sense, Tilly's sardonic generalisation is certainly true for the majority. Most people in Dungatar seem to focus on particular individuals whom they 'love to hate' and, although the Dunnages are the town's primary target, they are not the only ones who trigger a negative response. Even Tilly, despite her craving for acceptance – 'But you want them to like you' – finally abandons all notions of goodwill and acts on the disgust she feels towards the townspeople. At the same time, there are a few exceptions who show instinctive, unfeigned benevolence towards all those around them.

Paragraph 1: Few of the characters in this text behave in a magnanimous way towards the Dunnages.

- Tilly's return to Dungatar opens up old wounds and prejudices. Note the general agitation on the first day she takes her mother into town: 'The nerve of that girl' (p.35).
- Tilly also evokes the townspeople's jealousy over her relationship with Teddy – 'They think I'm not doing you any good' (p.175).

- After Teddy's death, the town's hatred of the Dunnages intensifies – vilification of the pair spirals out of control.
- The townspeople are positioned to believe the worst and feed off each other: 'She made him jump … She is cursed' (p.201). Scapegoating the Dunnages provides a conduit for their anger and grief.

Paragraph 2: Ham suggests that the insular context of a small country town – where private lives are exposed and gossip is endemic – encourages intolerance.

- 'Everybody knows everything about everyone …' (p.33).
- A nosy, malevolent character like Beula Harridene has an extensive list of people whom she hates – Tilly is a 'murderess' (p.46), Teddy is 'a bludger and a thief' (p.28), and the rest of the town 'vile and repulsive' fornicators (p.96).
- In some cases, criticism is justified; for example, Elsbeth Beaumont's snobbery generates a collective desire to put her in her place.
- Equally, Trudy invokes the community's anger over her bullying during *Macbeth* rehearsals: 'You're not a very considerate director, *Gertrude*' (p.271).
- Parochialism is also a factor – Dungatar has a fierce rivalry with its neighbours, Winyerp and Itheca, especially on the football field.

Paragraph 3: Yet a handful of characters do not endorse the general narrative, and are motivated by charity rather than hate.

- When Tilly quotes from *Hamlet* – 'There is nothing either good or bad, but thinking makes it so' (p.175) – it is a reminder that people always have a choice about how they respond to others.
- Note Irma Almanac's and Mae McSwiney's small acts of charity to Molly Dunnage.
- Teddy shows kindness; for example, he finds a wheelchair for Molly and delivers it 'freshly scrubbed' (p.33) to the back door.
- Edward McSwiney is a decent, fair-minded man – he defends Tilly after Stewart's death, standing up to Evan Pettyman.

Paragraph 4: Sergeant Farrat – a genuinely empathetic individual – is the most singular example of goodwill in the text.

- He has a remarkably tolerant attitude to Beula Harridene – he even puts up with her smashing one of his headlights on the basis she is 'mad' (p.46).
- In the interests of community, he turns a blind eye to the pub's extended drinking hours.
- He is lenient with the little McSwineys.
- At Teddy's funeral, the sergeant speaks extensively about love and forgiveness; he tries to lead by example and diffuse the townspeople's irrational hatred for Tilly.
- He continues to support Tilly after she has been rejected by everyone else, bringing work for 'Dungatar's only real creative hands' (p.208).

Sample conclusion

Tilly's observation about hatred is based on the belief that people are judgemental by nature and will always find someone to criticise. Malicious tongues and unforgiving hearts are a toxic combination. Indeed, the novel concludes that most people actively derive pleasure from finding fault, relishing the sense of moral superiority that comes from disparaging their fellow human beings. This proclivity, regrettably, makes Dungatar a mean-spirited community. However, not everyone in the town is so uncharitable, and *some* characters resist this disagreeable aspect of human nature.

SAMPLE ANSWER

'In *The Dressmaker*, everyone has their place.' Do you agree?

Rosalie Ham's novel *The Dressmaker* is a scathing dissection of parochialism and narrow-mindedness. Dungatar is a tightly tiered society where, essentially, everyone has an allocated place. These rankings are dictated by wealth, occupation, convention and precedent. However, while Tilly's arrival is the catalyst that disrupts Dungatar's complacency, upsetting the status quo, the cracks are already evident. The text demonstrates that no community is impervious to shifts in the social order.

Theoretically, the Beaumont family of Windswept Crest – graziers with land and position – are at the top of the social ladder. Elsbeth Beaumont certainly considers herself superior to the locals whom she dismisses as 'un-refined'. When her son returns from his travels, she tells Muriel Pratt that William will need to look further than Dungatar in order to find 'suitable ... *companionship*'. Yet the once imposing family car is now 'tired' and Elsbeth's wardrobe seems to consist of a navy linen dress and a 'moth-eaten fox fur' that she wears with monotonous regularity. In reality, the Beaumonts are cash poor, and the townspeople, led by the Pratts (to whom Elsbeth owes money), see through her 'airs', treating her with thinly veiled scorn.

In Dungatar, money talks. Alvin Pratt, proprietor of the only general store in town, has done very well for himself and, although Elsbeth may disparage the family for moving in 'commercial circles' (p.119), Pratt has the upper hand. His decision to turn off the financial tap when his daughter and her new mother-in-law overspend in Melbourne leaves the Beaumonts in a compromising position. Nevertheless, even Pratt is not as rich as Evan Pettyman who, unbeknown to the rest of the town, subsidises his already-substantial income with criminal activities. Furthermore, Pettyman's role as shire president affords him added prestige and influence.

At the other end of the social scale is the family of Edward McSwiney, Dungatar's night cart man. They live humbly, with few possessions to call their own, not even a conventional house. In Dungatar, location reflects social status. Windswept Crest may have been rechristened Fart Hill by the locals, but it still physically stands above the town. By contrast, the McSwineys' compound, made up of abandoned railway carriages and damaged caravans, is positioned beside the tip.

Nevertheless, a community as self-righteous and inflexible as Dungatar is vulnerable to shake-up. The town's pre-ordained hierarchy is challenged by several individuals whose initiative and imagination empower them in unexpected ways. For example, Teddy has carved himself a distinctive niche, which enables him to transcend his lowly status as a McSwiney. He has proved himself both enterprising and useful by acting as Dungatar's social secretary and events manager, while his prowess on the football field has made him invaluable to the football-mad community.

Tilly's return to town introduces the alien concept of meritocracy. In ability and intelligence, Tilly is vastly superior to the people of Dungatar, but initially she resumes her designated role as outcast: 'That's Mad Molly's bastard girl'. Coupled with the tragedy of Stewart Pettyman's death, the Dunnages' flouting of convention has turned them both into social pariahs. In the pecking order, their rank is even lower than the McSwineys'.

However, preconceived attitudes can be overturned, particularly when self-interest is involved. Tilly's coveted talents as a dressmaker offer her a unique opportunity to make herself indispensable to the women of Dungatar. These women are so desirous of Tilly's skills that they are willing to set aside their historical grievances. As long as Tilly confines herself to making them beautiful clothes, their patronage, by definition, elevates her. It is when she oversteps the community-imposed boundaries and infiltrates the social sphere that she is brutally rejected. Dungatar's women only truly start to appreciate Tilly's worth when they discover the alternative is mediocrity. They have been spoilt by Tilly's excellence and, despite Una Pleasance's endorsement by the Pettymans, *Le Salon* is such a resounding failure that it is difficult for the women to pretend otherwise. Threatened with losing Tilly altogether to its rivals Winyerp and Itheca, Dungatar's former claim is reasserted by an insistent Trudy: 'She's ours'.

Events do not necessarily play out in a predictable way. Gertrude Pratt has no intention of accepting her place. Variously described as a 'heifer' by Elsbeth Beaumont and 'a great calico bag of water' by her father, Gertrude is given little chance of marrying anyone, 'least of all William Beaumont'. However, as 'Trudy' – and emboldened in no small part by Tilly's expertise – she successfully makes the leap from grocer's daughter to the wife of the heir to the largest estate in Dungatar. From Elsbeth's perspective, her son has married down but, motivated by ambition and fired with self-belief, Trudy has improved her social standing immeasurably. Conversely, Evan Pettyman's unanticipated downfall is spectacular – the once powerful councillor loses both his life and his reputation. Pettyman's demise is the result of his own perfidy and unscrupulous greed, but again, it also owes much to Tilly's intervention.

By the end of the novel, Tilly's destruction of the town has effected the ultimate shake-up; a cataclysmic upheaval that literally and metaphorically destroys all prior misconceptions as to who belongs where. When the townspeople, robbed of their homes and possessions, decide to appeal to Elsbeth Beaumont's largesse, the previous divide between 'the rabble' and the graziers of Windswept Crest is blurred. By converging en masse on the homestead, which still stands 'whole and perfect', the fates of everyone in Dungatar are unwillingly entangled.

The Dressmaker shows that, even in an apparently inflexible community like Dungatar, expectations can be overturned. Social mobility and social disgrace are both possible. Certain individuals – strong, clever, capable or ambitious – forge their own path, playing their cards in such a way that they rise above their previous station. Others become victims of their own weaknesses and lose everything. Irrespective of the hand these characters are originally dealt, their positions in society are not irreversible. Some do change places.

REFERENCES & READING

Text

Ham, R 2000, *The Dressmaker*, Duffy & Snellgrove, Sydney.

References and further reading

Clanchy, K 2015, '*The Dressmaker* by Rosalie Ham', *The New York Times*, 14 August, https://www.nytimes.com/2015/08/16/books/review/the-dressmaker-by-rosalie-ham.html

Ham, R 2020, *The Dressmaker's Secret*, Picador, Sydney.

Hoadley, N 2002, 'Interview with Rosalie Ham', *Steep Stairs Review*, 5 April, https://steepstairs.wordpress.com/2002/04/05/interview-with-rosalie-ham/

Latta, R 2015, 'A Review of *The Dressmaker* by Rosalie Ham', *Compulsive Reader*, 28 August, http://www.compulsivereader.com/2015/08/28/a-review-of-the-dressmaker-by-rosalie-ham/

Simmonds, D 2000, 'Review: *The Dressmaker* by Rosalie Ham', *The Weekend Australian*, 9 October, http://theweekendaustralian.com.au/arts/review-the-dressmaker-by-rosalie-ham

Steffens, D 2015, '*The Dressmaker* by Rosalie Ham', *The Boston Globe*, 21 August, http://bostonglobe.com/arts/books/2015/08/21/book-review-the-dressmaker-rosalie-ham/a3WMu6yQYgfvLHh8j8xA5H/story.html

The Dressmaker 2015, dir. Jocelyn Moorhouse, Apollo Media, Film Art Media and Screen Australia. Starring Kate Winslet, Liam Hemsworth, Judy Davis and Hugo Weaving.

Wilkes, J 2001, 'Rosalie Ham: *The Dressmaker*', *New Zealand Herald*, 22 June, https://nzherald.co.nz/lifestyle/irosalie-hami-the-dressmaker/QJNK3ZYQLCRMJBTETHOMVBUYAA/